THE VISION OF CATHOLIC SOCIAL THOUGHT

THE VISION OF CATHOLIC SOCIAL THOUGHT

THE VIRTUE OF SOLIDARITY AND THE PRAXIS OF HUMAN RIGHTS

MEGHAN J. CLARK

Fortress Press
Minneapolis

8666202144

THE VISION OF CATHOLIC SOCIAL THOUGHT

The Virtue of Solidarity and the Praxis of Human Rights

Data, charts, and case study information from the United Nations Development Programme (UNDP) are used with permission, courtesy of United Nations Development Programme.

Figure 1: "Ten Indicators" is taken from Alkire, S. and Santos, M. E. (2013) "Measuring Acute Poverty in the Developing World: Robustness and Scope of the Multidimensional Poverty Index". OPHI Working Paper No 59. http://www.ophi.org.uk/wp-content/uploads/ophi-wp-59.pdf. It is Used with Permission.

A portion of chapter four is a revised version of "Anatomy of a Social Virtue: Solidarity and Corresponding Vices"*Political Theology* 15. No1 (2014). Used with Permission.

Cover image: Fritz Eichenberg *Christ of the Breadlines*, 1950 (detail) / Wood engraving / Art © The Fritz Eichenberg Trust/Licensed by VAGA, New York, NY

Cover design: Laurie Ingram

Library of Congress Cataloging-in-Publication Data

print ISBN: 978-1-4514-7248-6

eBook ISBN: 978-1-4514-8440-3

The paper used in this publication meets the minimum requirements of American National Standard for Information Sciences — Permanence of Paper for Printed Library Materials, ANSI Z329.48-1984.

Manufactured in the U.S.A.

This book was produced using PressBooks.com, and PDF rendering was done by PrinceXML.

CONTENTS

Acknowledgements

It takes a community to raise a social ethicist, and in both my personal and professional life I have been formed by the witness and work of many others. This book is dedicated to the memory of my grandparents, John and Carol Clark. They took me to my first political protest, shopped with me for the local food pantry, and modeled faithful citizenship by explaining all of their activism for justice in light of the gospel. The Catholic faith passed on to me and my siblings during Sunday dinners is why I cannot stop blogging about Jesus and food stamps.

My sincerest gratitude goes to David Hollenbach, SJ. I thank him for his constant encouragement, challenging critiques, and generosity with his time and especially for his gracious foreword to this book. A special thanks as well to Elizabeth A. Johnson, CSJ, who inspired me as an undergraduate at Fordham University to pursue graduate studies in theology. At Fordham, her guidance and that of W. Norris Clarke, SJ, Joseph Koterski, SJ, Brian Davies, OP, Mark Massa, SJ, and Donna Mckenzie nurtured and urged me to pursue doctoral work. At Boston College, Lisa Sowle Cahill, Kenneth R. Himes, OFM, James Keenan, SJ, Stephen Pope, and Thomas Massaro, SJ, modeled a challenging and collaborative community. It was a privilege to learn to be an ethicist within such an encouraging and challenging community of scholars.

I am blessed to have wonderful colleagues and friends who provided much support as this book came to fruition. Warmest thanks to Teresa and Patrick Collins, Kevin Ahern, Amanda Osheim, Susan Frazzetto, Christopher Vogt, Patrick Flanagan, CM, Joann Heaney-Hunter, R. Ward Holder, Poppy Fry, Michael Jaycox, Nicholas Austin, SJ, Kimberly K. Asbury, and Monica Jalandoni for their friendship and willingness to read drafts, offer advice, and provide unconditional support. In the era of constant media and headlines, the need to bring Catholic theology into the public square is great, and I am lucky to have found a community of moral theologians at www.catholicmoraltheology.com and a forum for young Catholics voices at Millennial (www.millennialjournal.com). Being part of such diverse groups of scholars enriches my theology and vocation as a theologian. I am thankful to St. John's University for their institutional support through a yearlong research reduction as this book was being completed. In addition, St. John's faculty writing retreats led by Maura Flannery at the Center for Teaching and Learning and Anne Geller at the Faculty Writing Initiative were invaluable. At Fortress Press, Michael Gibson, Lisa Gruenisen, Jeremy Rehwaldt and others expertly guided this manuscript to publication.

In undergraduate and graduate studies, I suffered from debilitating migraine complications managed through the incomparable care of Dr. Mark Gudesblatt—I am immensely appreciative of all his diligence made it possible for me to accomplish.

This book is a labor of love for which the deepest thanks go to my family. My grandmother Joan McCarthy, aunts, uncles, and cousins provide an unconditional love and massive cheering section. Over the last two years, Hurricanes Irene and Sandy devastated my home in Long Beach, New York. Through the ups and downs of displacement, my sister and roommate Kaitlin also weathered the ups and downs of this book. I want to thank her and my brother Chip for always keeping me grounded and distracting me with Mets games. Finally, the person I am is thanks to my parents Drs. Charles and Lisa Clark. Their model of faithful service to one's family, the vulnerable and marginalized, and the church serves as a constant living example of striving to "live justly, love tenderly, and walk humbly with your God." Their personal and professional commitment to the common good motivates my own work. My father is an accomplished economist committed to Catholic social thought and poverty alleviation. With a doctorate and years as a nurse-practitioner, my mother tirelessly fights for the health and well-being of newborns at home and abroad. It is truly a wonderful gift to be able to collaborate with both of them in scholarship and an honor to be their daughter.

Foreword

David Hollenbach, SJ

Meghan Clark's *Vision of Catholic Social Thought* gives us a compelling approach to key ethical issues that are arising in the context of our globalizing world. Globalization is having an increasingly powerful impact on many of the political, economic, and cultural realities shaping the lives of men and women today. Globalization has been described by Robert Keohane and Joseph Nye as the increase in networks of interdependence among people at multicontinental distances.[1] This description of globalization as a network highlights the fact that it is not a single strand of interconnection such as increased trade or financial interchange. It is occurring on multiple levels of social life—the political, the cultural, the technological, and the environmental.

This thickening network of interdependence affects human well-being both for ill and for good. Ill effects such as the continuing poverty of so many in the developing world, especially sub-Saharan Africa, are often at the center of the discussions of those working for justice in church-related social action agencies and in secular activist groups as well. In these settings globalization is often seen as the expansion of Northern influence upon the less-powerful nations of the global South that keep them in poverty. In this perspective, globalization appears as itself a morally objectionable reality. It is a form of interconnection in which emerging economic, political, and cultural interconnections among peoples become forms of domination. There can be no doubt that such patterns of domination far too often mark the new interconnections emerging among the nations and peoples in the world today.

A second approach to the developments occurring in our increasingly interconnected world has been proposed by Roland Robertson. Robertson notes that this growing interconnection is giving rise to a new awareness that all people genuinely share the same time and the same space, the same history and the same world, the same earth. Used this way, the term *globalization* points to a new kind of human consciousness: an intensified awareness of the unity of the world as a whole that takes the globe itself as a framework for human

1. Robert O. Keohane and Joseph S. Nye, "Globalization: What's New? What's Not? (And So What?)" *Foreign Policy*, no. 118 (Spring, 2000): 104–19, at 105.

activities.[2] Globalization thus leads people to an increased recognition that they are part of a single community bound together in what can be called de facto interdependence.

This awareness of our de facto interdependence raises a moral challenge. It calls those who recognize they are bound together by new patterns of global trade, finance, and environmental links to recognize that they also have mutual moral responsibilities toward each other. In the words of Pope John Paul II, these factual linkages point to "the need for a solidarity which will take up interdependence and transfer it to the moral plane."[3] Thus, globalization can move from being used to express negative judgments of domination of the poor by the rich, to pointing to of new factual forms of global interconnection, to serving as a moral concept that highlights the growing need for responsibility in mutual solidarity across the boundaries that divide the planet.

The challenge, of course, is whether global solidarity based on mutuality and equality will shape the factual patterns of global interdependence that are growing in our world. If this does not happen, then increasingly the term *globalization* will point to domination of the poor by the rich and the weak by the strong. But if contemporary consciousness is further shaped by the awareness not only that all human beings inhabit the same history and the same planet but that they are members of a single human family with mutual responsibilities toward one another, then *globalization* can become a term used to describe a morally valuable development in human history.

Meghan Clark explores the resources within recent Catholic social thought that can help promote the move from a kind of global interdependence that is unjust and exploitative to one marked by greater justice and peace. She mines the long Catholic tradition and shows how its understanding of the essential linkage between the good of the human person and the common good of society points the way to a just form of globalization. This linkage of personal and common goods is at the basis of recent Catholic insistence that participation in the economic and political life of society is essential to the realization of the dignity and freedom of the person. No person is an island, so solidarity with others is a precondition for personal fulfillment.

Clark shows how this social understanding of personhood shapes a vision of development that can energize a move from unjust to just patterns of globalization. She also presents a powerful interpretation of human rights that

2. Roland Robertson, *Globalization: Social Theory and Global Culture* (London: Sage, 1992), 8.

3. John Paul II, *Sollicitudo Rei Socialis*, no. 26. This encyclical, issued in 1987, is available on the Holy See's website, at http://www.vatican.va/holy_father/john_paul_ii/encyclicals/documents/hf_jp-ii_enc_30121987_sollicitudo-rei-socialis_en.html.

will advance this move to greater justice. The vision she draws from Catholic social thought is compassionate, demanding, and presented with intellectual care. Let us hope that this book will lead many to see the world in the way Clark's vision suggests, and to act in ways suggested by this vision as well.

David Hollenbach, SJ
University Chair in Human Rights and International Justice and Director of the Center for Human Rights and International Justice
Boston College
Chestnut Hill, MA

Catholic Social Teaching Documents and Abbreviations

In Chronological Order

RN   *Rerum Novarum (On the Condition of Labor)* Pope Leo XIII, 1891

QA   *Quadragesimo Anno (After Forty Years)* Pope Pius XI, 1931

MM   *Mater et Magistra (Christianity and Social Progress)* Pope John XXIII, 1961

PT   *Pacem in Terris (Peace on Earth)* Pope John XXIII, 1963

GS   *Gaudium et Spes (Pastoral Constitution on the Church in the Modern World)* Vatican II, 1965

PP   *Populorum Progressio (On the Development of Peoples)* Pope Paul VI, 1967

OA   *Octogesima Adviens (A Call to Action on the Eightieth Anniversary of Rerum Novarum)* Pope Paul VI, 1971

JM   *Justitia in Mundo (Justice in the World)* Synod of Bishops, 1971

LE   *Laborem Exercens (On Human Work)* Pope John Paul II, 1981

SRS   *Sollicitudo Rei Socialis (On Social Concern)* Pope John Paul II, 1987

CA   *Centesimus Annus (On the Hundredth Anniversary of Rerum Novarum)* Pope John Paul II, 1991

CV   *Caritas in Veritate (Charity in Truth)* Pope Benedict XVI, 2009

Other Encyclicals:

RH   *Redemptor Hominis (On the Redeemer of Man)* John Paul II, 1979

DCE   *Deus Caritas Est (God Is Love)* Pope Benedict XVI, 2005

SS   *Spe Salvi (On Hope)* Pope Benedict XVI, 2007

LF   *Lumen Fidei (Light of Faith)* Pope Francis, 2013

Unless otherwise noted, all encyclicals and quotations can be found at online at vatican.va.

Introduction: The Vision of Catholic Social Thought

"Whereas recognition of the inherent dignity and of the equal and inalienable rights of all members of the human family is the foundation of freedom, justice and peace in the world."
    Universal Declaration of Human Rights of 1948, Preamble

"Social justice and social charity must, therefore, be sought. . . . [T]he institutions themselves of peoples and, particularly those of all social life, ought to be penetrated with this justice. . . . Social charity, moreover, ought to be as the soul of this order."
    Pope Pius XI, Quadragesimo Anno 88

In the face of twentieth-century horrors, from the Shoah to Rwanda, Darfur to Syria, apartheid to the factory-fire massacre in Bangladesh, the language of human rights has emerged as compelling rhetoric and framework. Our social conscience struggles with the expanding recognition of the humanity of all peoples and the ambiguity of the claims the suffering of others places upon us. The last century marked the spread of liberation movements and the enculturation of human rights. Rights are the primary framework and language for global ethics discussions within the international community. Despite ongoing and significant debates about what constitutes human rights, the concept currently commands a pride of place at the United Nations as the vocabulary and structure for addressing ethics in international debate. Development, poverty, peace building, responses to violence—the list of pressing global social concerns dependent upon the human rights project is long.

What, though, are human rights? The term is used so frequently and casually that they seem all encompassing and elusive. Who "has" them? Individuals? Communities? In popular discussion, the term *right* is broadly used to identify those services or protections one can lay claim to in society (the right to freedom of speech, movement, education, access to health care, and so on). This text will identify a right as having three distinct elements. A right begins with a person who is the bearer of the right (subject) and includes a particular substance (object) that is claimed against another individual or group who has the correlative duty to respect this right. For example, the right to freedom of speech is a right of an individual to speak his or her mind freely without interference from other individuals or groups. Moreover, the protection of this right, the locus of the duty, is often understood in terms of the legal guarantee by the state (as part of the basic framework of law within a community). In particular, contemporary legal recognition of these rights begins with the Universal Declaration of Human Rights and the particular emphasis of the United Nations of codifying human rights within national and local laws.

Within human rights discourse, human rights are often pitted against any substantive understanding of the community, the common good, or solidarity. Throughout the Cold War, in particular, strong dichotomies between international treatment of civil-political rights and social, economic, and cultural rights. Globally, "Western human rights," because of their liberal and individual emphasis, have come under fire from a variety of non-Western scholars: African, Islamic, Confucian, Buddhist, and so on. African political scientist Claude Ake argues that the liberal human rights tradition is sociologically specific and that African communities "have little interest in choice for there is no choice in ignorance. There is no freedom for hungry people, or those eternally oppressed by disease. It is no wonder that the idea of human rights has tended to sound hollow in the African context."[1] Ake and others who critique the Western human rights tradition acknowledge that political liberties are necessary; however, they are not the ultimate goal. In addition, the individual focus of human rights is critiqued as contrary to "Asian values" that prioritize the community (this applies to African cultural critiques as well).

Answering these critiques, contemporary human rights scholars and activists have sought to reclaim the unity of the Universal Declaration of 1948 and develop the inclusive force of human rights theory. As Ake argues, "human rights will play their proper role in social development in Africa today only when they are conceived as the Universal Declaration understood them fifty years ago—as including both civil-political and social-economic rights."[2]

1. Claude Ake, "The African Context of Human Rights," in *Applied Ethics: A Multicultural Approach*, ed. Larry May et al. (Upper Saddle River, NJ: Prentice Hall, 1994), 95.

2. David Hollenbach, SJ, *The Global Face of Public Faith: Politics, Human Rights and Christian Ethics* (Washington, DC: Georgetown University Press, 2003), 228.

One example of this shift toward an integrated approach focused on basic necessities and the community is the work of the United Nations Development Programme (UNDP). Through the human development reports of the last decade, UNDP attempted to integrate the human rights project with attention to both individuals and communities—offering an integrated view of human development. Entering into this conversation, this book offers a vision of Catholic social thought as providing an understanding of human rights and solidarity in which the individual and community are respected. For Catholic social thought, human rights and solidarity cannot be at odds, as one cannot truly be present without the other. The two are intrinsically connected in the human person and mutually dependent upon one another for fulfillment.

WHAT IS CATHOLIC SOCIAL TEACHING?

In November 2012, a fire broke out in a clothing factory in Dhaka, Bangladesh, killing more than one hundred factory workers, who were working in unsafe conditions for virtually nothing.[3] The fire shocked people around the world. In Bangladesh, people protested and marched, demanding safer working conditions. Around the world, petitions emerged, demanding American and European companies (Walmart and the Gap in particular) take responsibility for working conditions along their supply chain. Then, in May 2013, when asked to comment on workers protesting the lack of changes in Bangladesh, Pope Francis condemned the treatment of Bangladeshi factory workers as *slave labor* that goes against God but produces cheap goods for the developed world.[4] It is within a similarly complex reality of exploitation, injustice, and movements for justice that modern Catholic social teaching emerged in 1891. The nineteenth century brought with it rapid social, political, philosophical, and economic changes. In particular, the rise of factories, exploitation of workers, and emergence of communism and socialism called for new social reflection. Thus, modern Catholic social teaching emerged as a response when Pope Leo XIII issued *Rerum Novarum* (*On the Condition of Labor*) in 1891.[5] Rooted in the

3. "Dhaka Bangladesh Clothes Factory Fire Kills More than 100," *BBC News*, 25 November 2012, http://www.bbc.co.uk/news/world-asia-20482273.

4. Krishnadev Calamur, "Pope Compares Bangladesh Factory Conditions to Slave Labor," *The Two-Way: Breaking News from NPR*, National Public Radio, May 1, 2013, http://www.npr.org/blogs/thetwo-way/2013/05/01/180406283/pope-compares-bangladesh-factory-workers-to-slave-labor.

5. For more on this see Jean-Yves Calvez, SJ, and J. Perrin, SJ, *The Church and Social Justice* (Chicago: Henry Regnery, 1961) Charles E. Curran, *Catholic Social Teaching 1891–Present: A Historical, Theological and Ethical Analysis* (Washington, DC: Georgetown University Press, 2002); Kenneth R. Himes, OFM, et al. *Modern Catholic Social Teaching: Commentaries and Interpretations* (Washington, DC: Georgetown

long-standing tradition of Christian moral reflection, Catholic social teaching adapted and developed the church's social doctrine through direct and systematic engagement with new social problems through a series of papal encyclicals, conciliar and synodical documents, and episcopal statements. All of the popes from John XXIII to Benedict XVI have developed and emphasized Catholic social teaching through their encyclicals. While he has not yet offered a social encyclical, Pope Francis's contribution to Catholic social teaching is anticipated with great expectation. And as his statements in response to the situation of Bangladeshi factory workers indicate, the exploitation of workers and the human dignity of those on the margins of society remains as much a focus in Catholic social teaching as it did in 1891.

Frequently called Catholicism's *best kept secret*, Catholic social teaching is the church's explicit and official grappling with contemporary social problems. While initially employing faith and reason to provide moral guidance to all the faithful, beginning with Pope John XXIII, the tradition explicitly engaged not only the Catholic Church but all people of goodwill. Today, Catholic social teaching is a primary resource for the Catholic contribution to the public sphere on matters of globalization, justice, human dignity, and peace. Catholic social thought, on the other hand, refers to the reflections, analysis, and social ethics by theologians and other scholars in light of Catholic social teaching. Johan Verstraeten explains, "The Catholic social tradition can be interpreted as a tradition which comprises a particular set of shared understandings about the human person, social goods, and their distributive arrangements. This particular understanding is grounded in a living relation to the constitutive narratives provided by the Bible, integrated in a theoretical framework which makes it possible for the catholic understanding to remain open to rational explanation and public debate."[6] This encompasses not only the Catholic theological tradition but also the work of philosophers, sociologists, economists, and the like. Catholic social thought is the broad tradition of theologians, intellectuals, activists, social movements, and others responding to the *signs of the times*. This book is an example of Catholic social thought on human rights and solidarity as they developed in the last fifty years of Catholic social teaching.

University Press, 2004)' Joe Holland, *Modern Catholic Social Teaching: The Popes Confront the Industrial Age, 1740–1958* (New York: Paulist, 2003) Jack Mahoney, SJ, *The Challenge of Human Rights: Origin, Development and Significance* (Oxford: Blackwell, 2007); and Marvin Krier Mich, *Catholic Social Teaching and Movements* (Mystic, CT: Twenty-Third, 1998).

6. Johan Verstraeten, "Re-Thinking Catholic Social Thought as Tradition," in *Catholic Social Thought: Twilight or Renaissance?*, ed. J. S. Boswell, F. P. McHugh, and J. Vertraeten (Leuven: Leuven University Press, 2000), 64.

Over the last fifty years, this teaching has relied on two distinct yet related themes in its analysis: human rights and solidarity. Despite their prominence, the relationship between solidarity and human rights is left largely unexamined. What is the relationship between human rights and solidarity? This book aims to answer this question through a systematic investigation of recent Catholic social teaching, and it makes a constructive argument for the philosophical and theological anthropology behind the prioritization of human rights and solidarity. Human rights and solidarity do not emerge as twin pillars of Catholic social teaching by accident but because the two are intricately linked in the human person. Through the theme of integral human development and a dialogue with social analysis, this book further shows that connecting human rights and solidarity is necessary for both expanding human rights and building community. Through explicating the virtue of solidarity and its corresponding vices, this book argues that solidarity is a social virtue that is cultivated and habituated through the practice of respect for human rights. The vision of solidarity and human rights in Catholic social thought, then, contributes to and can help clarify the wider secular debates concerning the future of the human rights project, specifically broadening responsibility for human rights,clarifying and supporting the emerging responsibility to protect doctrine, and structuring just partnerships for development.

OUTLINE OF CHAPTERS

The first chapter, "Catholic Social Teaching on Human Rights and Solidarity," examines in depth the development of human rights and solidarity over the last fifty years. Beginning with Pope John XXIII, Vatican II, and Pope Paul VI, human rights and solidarity are introduced into the tradition and quickly rise in prominence. Using personalism as his frame, Pope John Paul II develops solidarity; however, the concrete parameters of solidarity and its relationship to human rights remain unexamined. Finally, Pope Benedict XVI's *Caritas in Veritate* (2009) uses charity as its primary theological lens while maintaining the central prominence of human rights and solidarity. As Catholic social teaching develops, a defined and clear tradition of human rights emerges beside an evolving and ambiguous theology of solidarity. For the purposes of scope, this book is limited to papal social encyclicals and council and synod documents. It does not address the numerous contributions of national or regional episcopal conferences. Starting with John XXIII, Catholic social thought adapts and adopts human rights language. Its use of human rights has expanded, influenced the wider human rights tradition, and emerged as a strong, well-defined approach. Solidarity, on the other hand, emerges slowly—as an attitude, a duty, a feeling, and finally a virtue. In contrast to most treatments of solidarity that focus only on John Paul II, this chapter places the emergence of solidarity as a virtue in John Paul II's thought within the context of what came before and after. Through a detailed examination of the insights and ambiguities of these two themes, this chapter lays the foundation for the connection of human rights to solidarity forwarded in the rest of this book.

In order to examine the relationship between human rights and solidarity, chapter 2, "Anthropological Foundations for Human Rights and Solidarity," turns to the human person as the foundation for both human rights and solidarity. Both human rights and solidarity hinge on the view of the person—human rights require a view of the person as fundamentally linked with others, and solidarity mandates respect and promotion of human rights. The legacy of the Enlightenment—in particular, one of its heroes, Immanuel Kant—placed great emphasis on the individual and an individual understanding of rationality and autonomy. This chapter argues this is not a sufficient view of the human person for understanding human rights and solidarity. Instead, I argue, through an explication of philosophical and theological anthropology, that both human rights and solidarity are required by the integrated and relational view of the human person. Using the moral philosophy of Charles Taylor, I offer an account of socially embedded agency, freedom, and the fundamental recognition of the equal humanity of other persons as the normative basis for the person's authentic participation in community. This understanding of the person highlights a normative link between solidarity and human rights, exhibited in Taylor by the obligation to belong. Beyond the philosophy of the person, Catholic social teaching's commitment to human rights and solidarity is based on a particular theological foundation. Theologically, the link between solidarity and human rights lies within the human person as created in the image and likeness of God (*imago dei*). To be in the image and likeness of God includes our relational nature, and for Christian theology our relational nature is in the image and likeness of the Trinity. *Imago dei* then must also be *imago trinitatis*. This relationality and emphasis on community is central to our theology of the person, creation, and covenant. Using the contemporary Trinitarian theologies of Catherine Mowry LaCugna and Elizabeth A. Johnson, CSJ, this chapter argues that just as *I* am in the image of God, so too *we* are in the image of God. The relationality of the Trinity, then, is important for our understanding of solidarity. Based on the equality, mutuality, and reciprocity of the Trinity, then, we as community image God in the world—more or less fully—through living solidarity and human rights.

A common critique of Catholic social teaching is that it is naive and overly optimistic in its approach. The third chapter, "Integral Human Development, Practicality, and Social Analysis," begins with Catholic social teaching's approach to development. The human right to development was recognized and examined in Catholic social teaching twenty years before its addition to the United Nations canon. It is primarily a communal and not an individual right. For decades, development was not viewed through human rights but was seen purely as a matter of economics and numbers. This changed in recent decades through the theoretical work of scholars like Nobel laureate Amartya Sen and programs like the Millennium Development Goals at the United Nations. In dialogue with the social analysis of Sen and the Millennium Development Goals data, this chapter examines the capabilities, substantive freedoms, and advances made through an integrated approach to development. While it provides important context, the approach taken by Sen and the United Nations Development Programme alone is not sufficient, as it still primarily offers a functional understanding of community. Despite the great progress toward a more integrated view of development, Sen and others still lack a substantive view of the community capable of solidarity. This is precisely what the vision of Catholic social thought offers to all people of goodwill. In the pursuit of development as a human right, Catholic social teaching offers a virtue of solidarity that goes beyond treating the community as an instrument for human rights. Thus, the virtue of solidarity here enhances Sen's understanding of human rights. The social virtue of solidarity linked to human rights and rooted in a relational anthropology is an important contribution of Catholic social thought to human rights discourse.

Returning to Catholic social teaching, chapter 4, "The Virtue of Solidarity and the Praxis of Human Rights," provides a detailed exposition of the virtue of solidarity as habituated through the praxis of human rights. This chapter pulls together the analysis of the first three chapters by offering a constructive framework for solidarity. Focusing in detail on three levels of solidarity—as an attitude, a duty, and a virtue, which emerge from the exposition in the first three chapters—this chapter attempts to clarify and concretize Catholic social teaching's understanding of solidarity. If solidarity is a social virtue, then what are the specific parts of the virtue? Does it have corresponding vices? And what are the practices by which individuals and communities habituate the virtue? This chapter provides a detailed theory of solidarity as a virtue and its cultivation through practicing respect for human rights. It also places solidarity in conversation with justice, a related yet distinct virtue. Furthermore, understanding solidarity as a virtue between vices provides a new interpretive lens for situating the current focus on human rights and solidarity within the broader tradition's search for the common good and its rejection of multiple forms of individualism and collectivism.

The final chapter, "Engaging the Future of the Human Rights Project and Building Solidarity," briefly identifies how the vision of Catholic social thought detailed in this book can provide important insights for rethinking responsibility for human rights within the context of globalization. Where secular human rights discourse has focused on the individual and located responsibility primarily in the civil authority of the nation-state, the vision of Catholic social thought integrates human rights and solidarity beginning with the human person. While responsibility is located in the nation-state, the centrality of the one human family for both human rights and solidarity provides a wider framework of responsibility, which is critical for three ongoing international debates. First is the debate concerning responsibility for human rights and transnational actors. What is the responsibility of a transnational corporation or nongovernmental organization (NGO) for promoting human rights? The second is the responsibility-to-protect doctrine, which moved to the international spotlight in 2012 through the events in Libya and elsewhere. What is the responsibility of the international community for human rights when a people suffer human rights violations either at the hands of their own government or their government's inability to protect them? Finally, as development is a primary focus of the global agenda and as we move from the Millennium Development project toward new *sustainable development goals* in 2015, how do we create partnerships for development that respect human rights and build solidarity? Can a just partnership exist between developed and developing countries, groups, or NGOs?

Ultimately, this book argues that participation is absolutely crucial for both human rights and solidarity. The radical claim of Catholic social thought is not that you and I both have equal humanity or human dignity. The radical claim of Catholic social thought is that my humanity is bound up in yours. We are one, such that when your human rights are violated, my dignity is violated as well. The virtue of solidarity pushes us to build a fully human community through practicing respect for human rights. This vision can offer a significant contribution to ongoing debates about the role of community in human rights. For Catholic social thought, it is a matter of living more fully human lives in the world, to more fully seek Jesus' prayer in John's Gospel "that they may be one" (17:20-21) through our participation in the humanity of one another.

1

Catholic Social Teaching on Human Rights and Solidarity

"Beginning our discussion of the rights of the human person, we see that everyone has the right to life, to bodily integrity, and to the means which are suitable for the proper development of life; these are primarily food, clothing, shelter, rest, medical care and finally the necessary social services."
Pope John XXIII, Pacem in Terris 11

"There can be no progress towards the complete development of the human person without the simultaneous development of all humanity in the spirit of solidarity."
Pope Paul VI, Populorum Progressio 43

At the end of World War II, the world order as it had existed was in shambles. The unspeakable horror and devastation of both the Holocaust and the war itself required a global response. Though this is the period of growing Cold War alliances, 1948 also marked the emergence of a new social and political order with the United Nations and the Universal Declaration of Human Rights. While the Catholic Church and Catholic intellectuals were deeply involved with both developments, the official moral teaching of the Roman Catholic Church did not then embrace the language of human rights.[1] Catholic moral

---

1. For a full treatment of these developments, see Mary Ann Glendon, *A World Made New: Eleanor Roosevelt and the Universal Declaration of Human Rights* (New York: Random House, 2001); Jacques Maritain, *Man and the State* (Chicago: University of Chicago Press, 1951; repr., Washington, DC: Catholic University Press, 1998); David Hollenbach, SJ, *Claims in Conflict: Retrieving and Renewing the Catholic Human Rights Tradition* (New York: Paulist, 1979); and Jack Mahoney, SJ, *The Challenge of Human Rights: Origin, Development and Significance* (Oxford: Blackwell, 2007).

theology preferred the language of natural law, in which the church sought to discover and explain moral laws based upon relationships within the created world.[2] During the 1960s there was a significant shift toward the language of human rights through the teachings of Pope John XXIII, Vatican II, and Pope Paul VI. Beyond the inclusion of human rights language, this period also marked the development of Catholic social teaching on solidarity. Deepening and expanding the centrality of human rights and solidarity, the papacy of John Paul II from 1978 to 2005 continued the social message of his recent predecessors, infusing it with a personalist philosophy. This process continued with Pope Benedict XVI, who further developed the tradition on human rights and solidarity through the lens of charity. This chapter traces the prioritization and development of human rights and solidarity, highlighting key insights and lasting ambiguities that emerge within the tradition. Both human rights and solidarity are recognized as central to any comprehensive response to global problems. However, deep ambiguity remains concerning solidarity, and yet solidarity is the necessary companion of human rights.

The Turn toward Human Rights and Solidarity: John XXIII, Vatican II, and Paul VI

As a living tradition, Catholic social teaching develops and adapts to deal with emerging historical situations and the presence of new ethical concerns. Throughout their history, emerging Catholic social encyclicals use the vast wealth of Catholic moral theology to address new ethical situations in order to adapt the tradition and develop new ethical theories to deal with the problems of the modern world. Each encyclical builds on its predecessors as it moves forward. It would, therefore, be incorrect to imply that the concepts of human rights and solidarity are alien to the earlier encyclicals or that there is a lack of continuity in the tradition. Chronicling the development of Catholic human rights theory, David Hollenbach states that it "has roots all the way back to Thomas Aquinas, Augustine, the Bible and Aristotle. More proximately, it emerged from the social doctrine of the modern papacy."[3] While rooted in

---

2. A common example of this is Catholic social teaching's defense of private property in the early social encyclicals. For example, in 1931's *Quadragesimo Anno*, Pope Pius XI states, "The right to own private property has been given to man by nature or rather the Creator himself, not only in order that individuals may be able to provide their own needs and those of their families, but also that by means of it, the goods which the Creator has destined for the human race may truly serve this purpose" (QA 45). In this natural law understanding of the right to private property, the distinction is that private property is a derived right based on the universal destination of goods and the duty to provide for oneself and one's family. The right as such is not the primary or absolute goal.

this tradition, the writings of John XXIII, Vatican II, and Paul VI demonstrate a significant movement in both the theory and language of official Catholic social ethics. John XXIII's purpose and approach is rooted in his predecessors, yet he is the first pope to explicitly incorporate the language of human rights.[4] In addition, the language of solidarity evolves out of growing recognition of interdependence and its relation to the duty of the common good. During the decade from 1961 to 1971, the two are positioned as the two major pillars of an ethics for the contemporary world, though there is ambiguity in how and why the two are practically linked.

DEFINING AND GROUNDING HUMAN RIGHTS

In his 1961 encyclical, *Mater et Magistra* (*Christianity and Social Progress*), Pope John XXIII began to lay the foundation for the central mission of both *Pacem in Terris* (1963) and Vatican II (1960–1965), to reposition and refocus the engagement of the church in the many issues of the contemporary world—the Cold War, the nuclear arms race, and neocolonialism, among others. Examining this development in light of the growing complexity of the global sociopolitical situation, David Hollenbach explains:

> The consequence of this complexity is two-fold. First, human freedom is more and more both exercised and limited by social organization and government. Second, the process of social complexification threatens to undermine people's confidence in their ability to assume responsibility for their own lives. This process thus brings into question the transcendence of persons by threatening to subordinate them to the dynamics of social organization and government.[5]

Pope John XXIII's answer is a Catholic human rights theory built on the combination of rights and duties highlighted by his predecessors. All human rights are understood by John XXIII as applying to persons within communities. Reflecting back on *Rerum Novarum*, John XIII states that "private property, including that of productive goods, is a natural right possessed by all,

---

3. Hollenbach, *Claims in Conflict*, 41. For an extended examination of the development of Catholic human rights theory, see chapter 2.

4. Prior to John XXIII, Catholic social teaching focused on the natural law, which included both the right to property and an emphasis on duties; however, it intentionally avoided the specific language of human rights as evidenced in the United Nations Declaration of Human Rights.

5. Hollenbach, *Claims in Conflict*, 63.

which the state may by no means suppress. However, as there is from nature a social aspect to private property, he who uses his right in this regard must take into account not merely his own welfare but that of others as well" (MM 19). John is clearly and strongly reiterating the central concerns of Catholic social teaching: the dignity of the human person and the welfare of the community. This constant focus on both the person and community is further highlighted by his definition of the common good as embracing "the sum total of those conditions of social living, whereby men are enabled more fully and more readily to achieve their own perfection" (MM 65). True community, for John, exists "only if individual members are considered and treated as persons, and are encouraged to participate in the affairs of the group" (MM 65). Thus, John and his successor Paul VI develop a Catholic approach to human rights that includes all of the major hallmarks of the 1948 United Nations Declaration of Human Rights and expands this list significantly to include the rights and duties of individuals, communities, and nations, as well as the human right to development.

Explicit in its use of international human rights language, *Pacem in Terris* (*Peace on Earth*) is groundbreaking and controversial from its opening salutation. Traditionally, encyclicals had been addressed only to the Catholic hierarchy and faithful. The first encyclical addressed to non–Catholics, *Pacem in Terris* seeks to engage *all people of good will* on the heels of the Cuban Missile Crisis. While the subject of peace was not controversial, "the encyclical's recourse to rights' language itself constituted an intellectual challenge. For some it seemed a capitulation to the Enlightenment; to others it amounted to an overdue encounter with the secular (western) world."[6] However, in adopting the language of the UN Declaration of Human Rights, John was not capitulating but explicitly seeking a critical encounter with the secular world. *Pacem in Terris* adopts and adapts the rights found in secular rights theory and seeks to transcend the common political debates concerning the canon of human rights.

While much of the world was debating whether or not civil-political rights (those emphasized by Western democracies) or socioeconomic rights (those often associated with communism) were the primary or "real" rights, the actual cause of human rights suffered as a result. The UN declaration sought to transcend this debate by including all categories of rights and leaving it to the

6. Drew Christiansen, "Commentary on Pacem in Terris," in *Modern Catholic Social Teaching : Commentaries and Interpretations*, ed. Kenneth R. Himes, OFM, et al. (Washington, DC, Georgetown University Press, 2005), 224.

member states to implement and prioritize them. John XXIII, instead, sought to integrate and expand further the canon of human rights by offering a systematic listing of human rights and corresponding duties. Defining his starting point, John XXIII explains: "Any human society, if it is to be well ordered and productive, must lay down as a foundation this principle, namely, that every human being is a person; that is, his nature is endowed with intelligence and free will. Indeed, precisely because he is a person he has rights and obligations flowing directly and simultaneously from his very nature. And as these rights are universal and inviolable so they cannot in any way be surrendered" (PT 9). The divisions of Catholic human rights are not the polarized divisions between civil-political and socioeconomic rights. Instead, they are divided into three major categories: order between persons, between individuals and public authority within a state, and between states.

In the first section, *Pacem in Terris* details a very common list of the human rights of each and every individual human person. From the right to life and a worthy standard of living (PT 11), to freedom in seeking the truth (PT 12), to an education (PT 13), to active participation in political life (PT 26), to an opportunity to work, to a just wage and private property (PT 19–21), and to the right of meeting and association (PT 23–24), the individual rights enumerated are similar to those in any canon of human rights. However, as is characteristic of Catholic ethics, they are contextualized within the community and linked to associated duties. For example, while one has the right to active participation in the political life of the community, "the fact that one is a citizen of a particular state does not detract in any way from his membership in the human family as a whole, nor from his citizenship in the world community" (PT 25). While human rights apply to individual human persons, they are in no way individualistic. "The natural rights with which we have been dealing are, however, inseparably connected, in the very person who is their subject, with just as many respective duties. . . . [T]he right of every man to life is correlative with the duty to preserve it; his right to a decent standard of living with the duty of living it becomingly" (PT 28, 29). The rights one holds as an individual human person cannot be properly understood without the responsibilities attached to those rights.

Recognizing and living out one's own individual human rights is not sufficient; all human rights include the primary duties of reciprocity and mutual collaboration. Founded on the equality of all human persons, human rights demand that when we recognize our own human rights, we have a duty to recognize the human rights of others; "once this is admitted, it also follows that in human society to one man's right there corresponds a duty in all other persons: the duty, namely, of acknowledging and respecting the right in question" (PT 30). To claim rights for oneself or one's own community but deny them to others is to "build with one hand and destroy with the other" (PT 30). Moreover, this duty is not abstract. John emphatically states, "It is not enough, for example, to acknowledge and respect every man's right to the means of subsistence if we do not strive to the best of our ability for a sufficient supply of what is necessary for his sustenance" (PT 32). We have a profound obligation to promote the human rights and flourishing of others as part of the common good. My own substantive exercise of my human rights is contingent on my striving for the substantive exercise of these rights for each and every individual human person and community. The practical application of this is evidenced throughout *Pacem in Terris*, in its attention to the interdependence of individuals and communities and its attempt to place relations between nations under the governance of human rights. Theologically and philosophically, however, the encyclical does not offer a developed foundation for why this is so.

Pacem in Terris goes beyond addressing the rights and duties of individuals to those associated with broader communal relationships. Where *Mater et Magistra* offers a clear definition of the common good with reference to both the community and each person within that community, John's treatise on human rights continues by addressing the relationship between individuals and the state. Human persons are social; they always live in communities. Therefore, they need civil authority: "Human society can neither be well-ordered nor prosperous unless it has some people invested with legitimate authority to preserve its institutions and to devote themselves as far as is necessary to work and care for the good of all" (PT 46). However, in accordance with the common good, this does not represent a blanket acceptance of all forms of authority. Legitimate authority, within the encyclical, is consistent with political participation in democracy as well as with civil disobedience against unjust laws and governments. Furthermore, the legitimacy of the civil authority is directly related to its protection and promotion of the human rights of its citizens or members (PT 60). A government that denies or violates the human rights of its citizens "not only fails in its duty, but its orders completely lack juridical force" (PT 61). The responsibility of the civil authority does not end with the nominal recognition of human rights, but extends to promoting the substantive value of these rights through social support and services (PT 56, 64). Employment is one area where the civil authority has expanded positive responsibilities for human rights: "the government should make similarly effective efforts to see that those who are able to work can find employment in keeping with their aptitudes and that each worker receives a wage in keeping with the laws of justice and equity" (PT 64). Without active support of the government, the substantive exercise of human rights is impossible for the marginal within society, as "inequalities between the citizens tend to become more and more widespread, especially in the modern world, and as a result human rights are rendered totally ineffective and the fulfillment of duties is compromised" (PT 63).

At the same time, the individual's right to political participation includes the duty to participate in the civil society: "it is in keeping with their dignity as persons that human beings should take an active part in government; although the manner in which they share in it will depend on the development of the country to which they belong" (PT 73). For example, the right to vote as a citizen (or most specifically the right to political participation) carries with it an implicit duty to vote or engage in oppositional protest as a form of political participation. Without baptizing a particular form and organization of civil government as divinely appointed, John defines legitimate civil authority in terms of human rights and the common good.

As persons, we are social beings who exist in various levels of community. Therefore, any understanding of human rights, from the perspective of Catholic social teaching, must be understood with reference to the community as a matter of the common good. The relationship between the individual and the state is to be judged, then, based on the promotion of human rights. The power and legitimacy of the government are directly related to its promotion of justice for its citizens through human rights, and human rights for the individual oblige participation in the civil society and political processes of the state. Expanding active participation is crucial to the evaluation of both. *Pacem in Terris* moves to the relations between states and argues that not only persons, but also nations, are the subjects of rights (PT 80). Framing his discussion of the relations between states within the framework of truth, justice, solidarity, and liberty, Pope John XXIII affirms, "All states are by nature equal in dignity. Each of them accordingly is vested with the right to existence, to self-development, to the means fitting to its attainment, and to be the one primarily responsible for this self-development." (PT 86). Just as it is the duty of individuals to recognize the rights of others, so too justice requires that states recognize the rights of others (PT 91). Rights and their respective duties always require mutuality and reciprocity (PT 92–93). Building on this, relations between states should be based on a working solidarity and in liberty, focusing on disarmament, freedom of states, and the centrality of the common good in relation to both their own citizens and other states.

Central to human rights, therefore, is its focus on duties or responsibilities. John succinctly argues, "if a man becomes conscious of his rights, he must become equally aware of his duties" (PT 44), including duties to himself or herself as well as to others. The attention to both human rights and their correlative duties is a defining characteristic of Catholic human rights theory and an important adaptation for our understanding of human rights. Catholic social teaching's understanding of the duty operates on three distinct yet related levels. First, an affirmation of human rights requires the duty of mutuality or reciprocity. On the individual level, this requires the recognition that if I claim human rights for myself, I must also recognize those rights for others. This duty of reciprocity is the context for duty within the UN declaration. This sense of duty, which addresses the *claim* of human rights, traditionally applied to the nation-state's legal recognition of these rights. Individuals have rights that they can claim against the state, which has the duty or responsibility to enforce them. In *Pacem in Terris*, however, this sense of duty applies to many levels: the individual, the state, and the international community.[7]

Second, there is a positive understanding of duty that goes beyond merely focusing on protecting individuals from having their rights directly infringed upon or violated. Duty here includes a positive requirement to promote human rights for oneself and others. It is not sufficient to acknowledge rights if we do not work for the exercise and substantive reality of these rights. While the role of the state is dominant in these matters, *Pacem in Terris* does not relinquish all responsibility for the duty of human rights to the state. Based on the principle of *subsidiarity*, which maintains that society should deal with situations on the lowest level possible but at the highest level necessary, the duty to actively create the conditions for greater exercise of human rights is the duty of individuals, families, communities, nations, and the international community. The state, then, is not necessarily the primary locus of the duties associated with human rights. The duty begins with the individual and extends to all levels, including the state and beyond. Finally, there is a correlative duty latent within the right itself. As stated, the right to life comes with a correlative duty to live life to the fullest. The freedom of choice is not the ultimate value. Human rights are understood as entitlements that carry a responsibility to human flourishing.

7. In its approach to the international community, *Pacem in Terris* receives a considerable amount of criticism for its idealism. The text envisions international structures that could enforce this larger duty of mutual respect for human rights in ways that did not exist at the time and still do not exist today. However, it is also a precursor to the development of the European Court of Human Rights and the International Criminal Court at The Hague. While neither of these function as John envisioned, they are developments in the direction of enforcing human rights.

Based on this, the next step after *Pacem in Terris* was the recognition of the right to development, the central theme for John's successor Paul VI. While the definition of integral development and solidarity is the subject of the next section, the listing of a right to development as a human right is a major addition in the Catholic human rights tradition and clearly points to the practical application of a focus on the community. Perhaps the clearest defense of the right to development as a central human right comes in the 1971 Synod of Bishop's statement *Justitia in Mundo* (*Justice in the World*), which states: "In the face of international systems of domination, the bringing about of justice depends more and more on the determined will for development. . . . This is expressed in an awareness of the right to development. The right to development must be seen as a dynamic interpenetration of all those fundamental interpenetration of all those fundamental human rights upon which the aspirations of individuals and nations are based" (JM 1.2). It is a clear example of a distinctive aspect of Catholic thought on human rights. As Kenneth R. Himes, OFM, notes, "it can be understood as an overarching category that includes many of the particular human rights endorsed by the Church" and necessary for a just structure of society.[8]

Recognized in Catholic social teaching more than twenty years before the United Nations acknowledged it as a human right, the right to development concretely illustrates that both individual persons and communities can be the subject of rights and of human dignity as understood both personally and communally.[9] This recognition of "*the dignity of the person in society*" leads John XXIII to focus on the common good and socialization, and to offer a canon of human rights that goes well beyond the rights of individuals.[10] This recognition also prompts Pope Paul VI to write two encyclicals addressing the concrete problem of authentic, equitable development: "The thread that ties all these rights together is the fundamental norm of human dignity. Human dignity is not an abstract or ethereal reality but is realized in concrete conditions of personal, social, economic and political life. The history of the papal teaching has been a process of discovering and identifying these conditions of human dignity. These conditions are called human rights."[11] Human rights and duties, then, are clarified by our understanding of the human person.

8. Kenneth R. Himes, OFM, "Commentary on *Justitia in Mundo* (*Justice in the World*)," in Himes et al., *Modern Catholic Social Teaching*, 343.

9. "United Nations Declaration on the Right to Development," 1986, un.org/documents/ga/res/41/a411/28.htm and ohchr.org/documents/issues/develop[pment/RTD_booklet_en.pdf

10. Hollenbach, *Claims in Conflict*, 66; emphasis added.

11. Hollenbach, *Claims in Conflict*, 68.

The strength of these early statements on human rights is in their concrete practical arguments. In particular, they adapt secular human rights language for a more integrated view of human rights applying to persons in communities and applying among communities, as well as a more complete understanding of duty or responsibility. The articulation of a right to development illustrates the centrality of the social situation and interdependence; however, these texts do not address the theological and anthropological foundations upon which the claims depend. This is a limitation of encyclicals in general: they do not develop the foundation. This is not a particular failure of *Pacem in Terris* as much as a limitation of encyclicals as a genre. Behind this integrated and communal approach to human rights, however, is an implicit theological and philosophical understanding of the human person. The understanding of the person in community leads to Catholic social teaching's emphasis on human rights and sparks the emergence of the theme of solidarity that follows.

INTERDEPENDENCE, DEVELOPMENT, AND SOLIDARITY

As secular ethics and society became more focused on the individual and individual freedom, Catholic social teaching emphasized the complexity of social relationships and the common good.[12] Without eliminating freedom, it develops an account of freedom within society through human rights but also by turning to solidarity as the answer to the complex social relationships of the modern world. However, unlike the detailed account of human rights, solidarity emerges as a much more diffuse and elusive concept.

Known for its definition of the common good, *Mater et Magistra* also briefly mentions the emerging theme of solidarity in response to the plight of agriculture workers (MM 146–48). Solidarity, as it develops, engages both persons and institutions. On the one hand, John XXIII argues for institutional support for agriculture, and, on the other, he encourages the cooperation and organizing of the farmers themselves. He states, "Indeed, it is proper for rural workers to have a sense of solidarity. . . . Finally, by acting thus, farmers will achieve importance and influence in public affairs proportionate to their own role. For today, it is unquestionably true that the solitary voice speaks as they say to the winds" (MM 146). In accordance with this, *Pacem in Terris* uses *active solidarity* as one of four organizing virtues—along with truth, justice, and

---

12. David Hollenbach explains: "1) human dignity is always supported, conditioned, and limited by the forms of social life within which it is found; 2) all arguments about the foundation of morality must take this social context of dignity into consideration as one of their starting points; and 3) the moral responsibility to the claim of worth of persons will be more and more mediated through social structures, even in 'the more intimate aspects of personal life.'" *Claims in Conflict*, 64.

liberty—governing the relations between states. Political leaders and citizens alike, we all "must remember that, of its very nature, civil authority exists not to confine its people within the boundaries of its nation, but rather to protect above all else, the common good of the entire human family" (PT 98). Thus, solidarity as the recognition that everyone must live together is a clear focal point for the argument for disarmament and against the arms race during the Cold War. In his book, *Catholic Social Teaching, 1891–Present,* Charles Curran points out that "here John XXIII substitutes solidarity for love, but this substitution makes sense because the topic involves the global relations between states."[13] However, while it applies to this context, it is not sufficient to understand solidarity simply as a placeholder for earlier discourses on love.

As it begins to emerge, solidarity has a political appeal: "Solidarity means recognizing that all political authority exists to fulfill the common good of the whole human family."[14] Whether aimed at moving the state to provide greater aid and services to its own rural farmers, or at convincing the community of nations that we belong to one human family and therefore the nuclear arms race poses a threat to all, solidarity points to the political and moral responsibility associated with both the domestic and universal common good. And yet, solidarity is not simply an ethical responsibility of the state, nor can it be fully understood within the realm of politics. The complex and multifaceted meaning and implications of solidarity are manifest in the myriad ways in which the term has been used throughout modern Catholic social teaching. Vatican II's use of solidarity in *Gaudium et Spes* (*Pastoral Constitution on the Church in the Modern World*) clearly illustrates the deep theological significance of solidarity beyond the responsibilities of the state. The document uses solidarity in three different contexts. First, similar to *Mater et Magistra* and *Pacem in Terris,* it states, "Although the world of today has a very vivid sense of unity and of how one man depends on another in needful solidarity; it is most grievously torn into opposing camps by conflicting forces" (GS 4). In a paragraph establishing the political and social context of the document, this use of solidarity is almost as a synonym for interdependence, as the council points to the same dangerous reality that prompted John XXIII's *Pacem in Terris.* Second, *Gaudium et Spes* points to the emergence of scientific study and the rise of a "sense of international solidarity, an ever clearer awareness of the responsibility of experts to aid men and even to protect them, the desire to make

13. Charles Curran, *Catholic Social Teaching 1891–Present: A Historical, Theological, and Ethical Analysis* (Washington, DC: Georgetown University Press, 2002), 74.

14. Christiansen, "Commentary on *Pacem in Terris*" 225.

the conditions of life more favorable for all" (GS 57). This growing sense of interconnectedness among the scientific and intellectual community is one of the positive values the council seeks to highlight from the modern world.

Instead of merely pointing to empirical *signs of the times*, the third use of solidarity in *Gaudium et Spes* points to the theoretical and theological foundation for this emerging call as an ethical imperative. In a section entitled, "The Incarnate Word and Human Solidarity," *Gaudium et Spes* 32 explicitly links solidarity with the theology of the *imago dei* and salvation history. Solidarity is not simply an empirical description of the modern world; it is also the way the world ought to be. According to the council:

> God did not create man for life in isolation, but for the formation of social unity. . . . So from the beginning of salvation history He has chosen men not just as individuals but as members of a certain community. Revealing His mind to them, God called these chosen ones "His people" (Ex 3:7-12) and even made a covenant with them at Sinai. This communitarian character is developed and consummated in the work of Jesus Christ. For the very Word made flesh willed to share in the human fellowship. . . . This solidarity must be constantly increased until the day on which it will be brought to perfection. Then, saved by grace, men will offer flawless glory to God as a family beloved of God and of Christ their Brother. (GS 32)

Vatican II clearly illustrates that solidarity is not simply a commentary on the signs of the times. Unlike interdependence, development, or increasing social complexity, solidarity develops as a theoretical way to understand many different aspects of the human person and the human reality. Not simply a reflection of the status quo, the call to solidarity is a normative theological reflection on the way human persons and human communities were created and intended to develop and flourish. To say that solidarity is an integral part of the very creation of human persons is furthermore to say that this intended solidarity is the way human communities *ought* to exist. *Gaudium et Spes* does not go any further in defining solidarity. It does, however, clearly illustrate that this solidarity is integral to the ethical involvement of Christians and the church within the modern world. Theologically, solidarity is beginning to be used in a broader sense. It is more than simply the statement that as human beings we are all part of the one human family. It is a call for that community to live and act in particular ways. To invoke creation, the incarnation, and God's covenant with the people is to call humanity to particular types of communities. This call goes beyond disarmament and an end to the Cold War.

Elaborating on solidarity and the many facets of the call to solidarity, Pope Paul VI turns his focus to development in his 1967 encyclical *Populorum Progressio* (*On the Development of Peoples*). From the first paragraph, Paul VI explains, "the demand of the Gospel makes it her duty to put herself at the service of all, to help them grasp their serious problems in all its dimensions, and to convince them that solidarity in action at this turning point in human history is a matter of urgency" (PP 1). Solidarity, as it is explicated in *Populorum Progressio*, is about integration and wholeness. "Development cannot be limited to mere economic growth. In order to be authentic, it must be complete, integral, that is, it has to promote the good of every man and of the whole man" (PP 14). Thus the distinction between authentic and inauthentic solidarity emerges in Catholic social teaching's contribution to debates concerning development.

Central to this connection between development and solidarity is Paul VI's argument that development touches all facets of human life—not only the economic and political. Solidarity applies to all persons, not only to political governments or individuals who are in leadership positions. Paul VI explains, "It is not just certain individuals, but all men who are called to this fullness of development. . . . We have inherited from past generations and we have benefited from the work of our contemporaries: for this reason, we have obligations toward all . . . the reality of human solidarity, which as a benefit for us also imposes a duty" (PP 17). Like the common good, development in solidarity must always attend to both each person and the community. Showing the deep influence of Catholic thinkers like Jacques Maritain, Paul VI is clear that development and solidarity are always both personal and communal; one cannot exist without the other in the common good. Adding to this, Paul VI speaks of the spirit of solidarity in which "there can be no progress toward the complete development of man without the simultaneous development of all humanity in the spirit of solidarity" (PP 43). What precisely is the spirit of solidarity? And what is the deeper reality out of which this spirit of solidarity is emerging? I contend that it is not sufficient to see this rising spirit of solidarity as merely the growing recognition that we live in an interdependent world; however, the reality of this interdependence is crucial for understanding the fundamental solidarity of humanity.

The strength of *Populorum Progressio* is its specificity, offering concrete ethical statements on how we should proceed in light of interdependence. In particular, it offers a specific understanding of the ethical obligations of solidarity. The obligation is threefold: "The duty of human solidarity—the aid that the rich nations must give to developing countries; the duty of social justice—the rectification of inequitable trade relations between powerful and weak nations; the duty of universal charity—the effort to bring a world that is more human toward all men, where all will be able to give and receive without one group making progress at the expense of another" (PP 44). Understood with justice and charity, solidarity is the duty of wealthier nations in relation to those underdeveloped nations. This duty, however, is not limited to nations; it is the same for each individual person as for larger political communities (PP 44). The emphasis within this document is the responsibility of developed nations to place their superfluous wealth at the service of the underdeveloped nations and the eradication of poverty in these countries. This is not, however, without its dangers, and one must remember that the duty of solidarity cannot be neocolonialism. Christian or authentic solidarity as it is being envisioned here is necessarily linked to justice in trade and charity. Whether it is being described as a spirit, an attitude, or a duty, equity and mutuality are hallmarks of solidarity in development. Allan Deck, SJ, clarifies, "In the task of pursuing a complete human development, the ability to enter into healthy dialogue with others is essential. That is the way to draw people and nations together in solidarity. That dialogue must first of all be based on the human person, not on commodities or things."[15] This is the strength of Paul VI's treatment of solidarity, and it is all building to Paul's final statement that development is the new name for peace.

Merely five years later, the 1971 Synod of Bishops picked up the theme of solidarity through development as the only way to peace in their letter *Justitia en Mundo* (*Justice in the World*). They begin: "The crisis of universal solidarity . . . economic injustice and lack of social participation keep man from attaining his basic human and civil rights."[16] In particular, they emphasize the right to participation for all members of the human family. Summarizing the teaching to date, they state, "*Pacem in Terris* gives us an authentic charter of human rights. In *Mater et Magistra*, international justice begins to take first place; it finds more elaborate expression in *Populorum Progressio*, in the form of a true and suitable treatise on the right to development."[17] A hallmark of the synod's document is its emphasis on education, justice, and solidarity. This education is

15. Allan Figueroa Deck, SJ, "Commentary on *Populorum Progressio* (*On the Development of Peoples*)," in Himes et al., *Modern Catholic Social Teaching*, 305.

16. *Justitia in Mundo*, in *Catholic Social Thought: the Documentary Heritage*, ed. David J. O'Brien and Thomas A Shannon (Maryknoll, NY: Orbis, 1992), 289.

17. Ibid., 297.

not limited to schools or formal learning but is an ongoing process throughout one's life, an education in human dignity and human rights. As Kenneth Himes explains, "This is an ongoing process leading to people becoming 'decidedly more human.' . . . [E]ducation for justice was education in solidarity; it must affirm the unity of humankind and bring people to work on behalf of that affirmation."[18] Human development here is more than mere survival; it is a process of becoming more fully human. Education in justice is an education in solidarity, and the crisis of solidarity is keeping human beings from attaining their basic human and civil rights. On a practical level, there is a deep unity of humanity, which is seen in the example of economic injustice and a lack of social participation, the answer to which is development. The practical application of solidarity, then, involves integral development in justice and participation. Solidarity, however, is not merely a synonym for development.

The right to development is recognized in Catholic social teaching almost twenty years before it appears in secular human rights theory because, as Himes notes, "human rights give specificity to the language of human dignity; they articulate the freedoms, the goods, and the relationships that are expressive of a person's dignity."[19] As stated earlier, *Pacem in Terris* presents a charter of rights, which taken as a whole represent the conditions necessary for the promotion and respect of human dignity. Thus, alongside the incorporation of a Catholic human rights theory emerged a theme of solidarity. Focused on the realities such as interdependence and sociality, solidarity became the recognition of human dignity within the community. In the spirit of solidarity or under the duty of solidarity, all nations and individuals are called to develop their own humanity through the recognition of that humanity in others. This is characterized as well through attention to the common good and the universal destination of goods. The theological and philosophical foundations for locating solidarity in the nature of the human person and communities are largely absent from these texts; in fact, the theoretical connection between human rights and solidarity is missing. What is the relationship between human rights and solidarity? More specifically, what are the implications of claiming that solidarity is a duty (a theme that itself needs greater development)? Here enters John Paul II and the exploration of human rights and solidarity through the lens of personalism.

18. Himes, "Commentary on *Justitia in Mundo (Justice in the World)*," 349.
19. Himes, "Commentary on *Justitia in Mundo (Justice in the world)* p. 343.

HUMAN RIGHTS AND SOLIDARITY IN THE PERSONALISM OF JOHN PAUL II

Under both John XXIII and Paul VI, Catholic social teaching developed in accordance with the ethical vision of these dynamic popes. Often considered his last will and testament, *Pacem in Terris* offered a defense of human rights from John XXIII's worldview. In the same vein, Paul VI sought to engage the contemporary scholarship on development and further his vision of a just development and peace. The election of Pope John Paul II, however, marked a transformation in Catholic social teaching's vision and perspective. In Karol Wojtyla, the church found a leader who was a philosopher and ethicist by training, a native of Poland who had lived under decades of an oppressive communist regime and who thus offered a more focused and theoretical defense of both human rights and solidarity. The philosopher pope, as he came to be known, went beyond his predecessors in personally shaping his social encyclicals. While, as pope, he begins laying out his theological and moral vision in his first encyclical *Redemptor Hominis* (*Redeemer of Man*), personalism is the ethical framework and contribution of John Paul II's social encyclicals. Central to this personalism is an emphasis on human dignity, human rights, and solidarity, as evidenced in his social encyclicals *Laborem Exercens* (*On Human Work*), *Sollicitudo Rei Socialis* (*On Social Concern*), and *Centesimus Annus* (*On the Hundredth Year*).

Personalism, as espoused by John Paul II, "is not primarily a theory of the person or a theoretical science of the person. Its meaning is largely practical and ethical: it is concerned with the person as a subject and as an object of activity, as a subject of rights, etc."[20] While it emerges out of a basic Thomistic metaphysical framework, Wojtyla's personalism is an active philosophy focusing on freedom and responsibility. He explains, "The person, therefore, is always a rational and free concrete being, capable of all those activities that reason and freedom alone make possible."[21] Instead of focusing on value or dignity, his personalism focuses directly on freedom and action. Freedom is the way in which human beings exist; it is the means of self-actualization. Therefore, "freedom is not given to us as an end in itself, but as a means to a greater end. . . . [F]reedom exists for the sake of morality and together with morality for the sake of a higher spiritual law and order of existence—the kind of order that most strictly corresponds to rational beings which are persons."[22]

---

20. Karol Wojtyla, "Thomistic Personalism," in *Person and Community: Selected Essays*, trans. Theresa Sandok, OSM (New York: Peter Lang, 1993), 165.

21. Ibid., 167.

22. Wojtyla, "Thomistic Personalism," 172.

All human beings have this capacity, even if they cannot at a given moment demonstrate it. This theory does not exclude in any way those who have not yet fully developed their rationality or those who can no longer exercise self-determination. Insofar as they are human beings and exist as human beings, they possess this human dignity and personal nature.[23] The human being is not simply an individual substance of a rational nature; he or she is a free agent, simultaneously subject and object of deliberate action.

Without continuing with an extensive philosophical investigation into the personalist philosophy of John Paul II, there are a few elements that are central to understanding the approach to both human rights and solidarity in his social encyclicals. As stated, he is highly concerned with the person as both the subject and object of activity. The person self-reveals in and through action. The starting point is an "experience of the human being in two senses simultaneously, for the one having the experience is a human being and the one being experienced by the subject is also a human being. The human being is simultaneously subject and object."[24] The human person, then, exists independently; however, it does not and cannot exist in isolation. For Wojtyla, the human person can only exist in relation to every other human person; thus, "one has to recognize everyone's fundamental right to act and thus everyone's freedom to act, through the exercise of which the self fulfills itself."[25] John Paul II's personalism, which borrows much from Kant, is a philosophy of the person articulated through an examination of the human act. Taking Kant's categorical imperative and adapting it to the gospel, he states, "Whenever a person is the object of your activity, remember that you may not treat that person as only the means to an end, as an instrument, but also allow for the fact that he or she too has or at least should have distinct personal ends. This principle, thus formulated, lies at the basis of all human freedoms."[26] Emphasizing the agent and the simultaneous focus on both the subjective and objective in human interaction, "this Personalism must not be confused with individualism. The human being is not a human person on one hand, and a member of society on the other. The human being as a person is simultaneously a member of society."[27]

Maintaining a balance between the individual and community is a hallmark of all of Catholic social teaching, and more broadly of Catholic

23. W. Norris Clarke, SJ, *Person and Being* (Milwaukee: Marquette University Press, 1993), 49.

24. Karol Wojtyla, "Person: Subject and Community," in *Person and Community*, 221.

25. Karol Wojtyla, *Towards a Philosophy of Praxis: An Anthology* (New York: Crossroad, 1981), 41.

26. Karol Wojtyla, *Love and Responsibility* (San Francisco: Ignatius, 1981), 28.

27. Karol Wojtyla, "The Problem of the Theory of Morality," in *Person and Community*, 146.

theology itself. While John Paul II's message is in deep continuity with his predecessors, he makes a slightly different and nuanced philosophical argument. In particular, he highlights freedom and agency and places them necessarily within the context of the common good. Participation is the key. Thus, he defines what it means to be *neighbor*, explaining that "as human beings we are capable of participation in the very humanity of other people, and because of this every human being can be our neighbor."[28] Thus, before becoming John Paul II, Wojtyla argues that an authentic community is one of solidarity. He defines this attitude of solidarity, stating: "The attitude of solidarity is a 'natural' consequence of the fact that a human being exists and acts together with others. Solidarity is also the foundation of a community in which the common good conditions and liberates participation, and participation serves the common good, supports it and implements it. Solidarity means the continuous readiness to accept and perform that part of a task, which is imposed due to the participation as member of a specific community."[29] As he examines solidarity in his philosophy, Wojtyla is clear that solidarity with others includes both accepting the duties and responsibilities imposed by the community and opposing unjust forms of exclusion and oppression.[30] While much more is required to do justice to Karol Wojtyla's personalism, the focus on participation and intersubjectivity is the context and background for the ethics of human rights and solidarity in his three social encyclicals.

From the beginning of *Laborem Exercens*, John Paul II's focus on the human person, as created in the image and likeness of God and called to work, is the starting point for his reflection on a theology and ethics of work. In his introduction, he states, "Thus work bears a particular mark of man and of humanity, the mark of a person operating within a community of persons" (LE 1). Furthermore, the person is the subject of work: "Because as the image of God, he is a person, that is to say, a subjective being capable of acting in a planned and rational way, capable of deciding about himself and with a tendency to self-realization. As a person, man is therefore the subject of

---

28. Karol Wojtyla, "Participation or Alienation?," in *Person and Community*, 201.

29. Wojtyla, *Toward a Philosophy of Praxis*, 47.

30. On one hand, he states, "The attitude of solidarity respects the limits imposed by the structures and accepts the duties that are assigned to each member of the community" (*Toward a Philosophy of Praxis*, 48); however, this is not meant to encourage complacency with unjust systems. Instead, Wojtyla explicitly states that authentic solidarity includes opposition. He explains, "Experience with diverse forms of opposition . . . teaches that people who oppose do not wish to leave the community because of their opposition. They are searching for their own place in the community—they are searching for participation and such a definition of the common good that would permit them to participate more fully and effectively in the community" (49).

work" (LE 6). So begins his treatise on the dignity and rights of workers (LE 1), arguing always that work is for the human person, not the human person for work (LE 6). Lamoureux explains, "At the core of LE and the context for understanding John Paul's agenda for social ethics is his theological anthropology. . . . The important insight of this encyclical is the integral connection between the person's self-realization and human labor."[31] Solidarity and the rise of solidarity movements (in Poland and around the world) provide the context for this encyclical. "It was the reaction against the degradation of man as the subject of work and against the unheard of accompanying exploitation in the field of wages, working conditions and social security for the worker. This reaction united the working world in a community marked by great solidarity" (LE 8). Thus, solidarity movements are about both solidarity and human rights. These movements, for John Paul II, emerge because of both the lack of community and the lack of respect for the human rights of workers.

The discussion of rights in *Laborem Exercens* reflects both the understanding of human rights of *Pacem in Terris* and the long-standing focus on the issue of private property from the beginning of the social encyclicals in 1891. While upholding the right to private property, John Paul reiterates that "the right to private property is subordinated to the right to common use, the fact that goods are meant for everyone. . . . The position of rigid capitalism must undergo continual revision in order to be reformed from the point of view of human rights, both human rights in the widest sense and those linked with man's work" (LE 14). Throughout this encyclical, the pope is clear that while he is arguing against communism, he is not by default offering blanket support of capitalism, which also has great dangers. While he specifically enumerates the various human rights associated with work (right to a just wage, right of association, and so on), these rights are always to be understood as parts of a greater whole. Referencing *Pacem in Terris,* he says, "The human rights that flow from work are part of the broader context of those fundamental rights of the person" (LE 16). For John Paul II, this is because we engage in self-actualization, develop our own personal freedom through work, and in an even broader sense through this process contribute to building an authentically human community. Within the context of work, the right to a just wage is one clear example of human rights as the necessary conditions of possibility for authentic human community.

---

31. Patricia Lamoureux, "Commentary on Laborem Exercens," in Himes et al., *Modern Catholic Social Teaching*, 394.

In developing his ethics of global solidarity, human rights are affirmed, but they are not significantly revised or expanded. In particular, John Paul II recognizes the growing awareness and support for human rights as a major positive development since *Populorum Progressio*, in which "the full awareness among large numbers of men and women of their own dignity and that of every human being" (SRS 26) emerged. It is through this form of participation that a human being recognizes his or her right and responsibility to live in the dialectic of solidarity and opposition. For John Paul II, solidarity does not exclude opposition; it can mandate it. Thus, he urges movements of solidarity to be open to dialogue (LE 8). Opposition to the state or other unjust social structures is a confirmation of both participation and the common good. This is because authentic opposition to social structure arises not from a desire to withdraw from the community and thereby deny the common good, but from an attempt to preserve it.[32] In many cases, "They are searching for their own place in the community; they are searching for participation and such a definition of the common good that would permit them to participate more fully and effectively in community."[33] Recognition of one's dignity and the dignity of all human beings is evidence of a deepening and fuller understanding of humanity. Thus, he concludes his reflections on the contemporary situation stating, "The awareness under discussion applies not only to *individuals* but also to *nations* and *peoples*. . . . [T]he *conviction* is growing of a radical *interdependence* and consequently of the need for a solidarity which will take up interdependence and transfer it to the moral plane. Today perhaps more than in the past, people are realizing that they are linked together by a *common destiny*, which is to be constructed together if catastrophe for all is to be avoided" (SRS 26). Therefore, the dynamics of both authentic solidarity and authentic opposition are included within solidarity.

And so begins John Paul II's examination of authentic human development, which always includes both solidarity and human rights. This "collaboration in the development of the whole person and of every human being is in fact a duty of all towards all and must be shared by the four points of the world: east and west, north and south" (SRS 32). It is a moral imperative that must include both solidarity and freedom to be authentically human. An individualistic, mechanistic, or consumerist development centered only on the individual can never be authentically human, "nor would a type of development which did not respect and promote *human rights*—personal and

---

32. Wojtyla, *Philosophy of Praxis*, 47.
33. Ibid., 49.

social, economic and political, including the rights of nations and peoples—be really *worthy of man*" (SRS 33). In a truly human ethical framework, human rights and solidarity are always simultaneously present. To be fully human requires both. Promotion of integral human rights is a necessary condition for the very possibility of authentic global solidarity. At the same time, to achieve the substantive mutuality and reciprocity required for universal human rights requires solidarity. Thus, the legal protection of human rights must not be limited to the developed "first world." The same human rights must be applied on the individual, communal, national, and international levels. Building from an established ethic of human rights, John Paul II turns to the moral dimensions of solidarity, which he characterizes as a reality, an attitude, a duty, and a virtue.

The twenty years between *Populorum Progressio* and *Sollicitudo Rei Socialis* involved a growing recognition of the interdependence of the entire human community. Interdependence, on every level of human society, is simply a reality of human existence. In Catholic social teaching, this reality is the experiential starting point for solidarity.

> It is above all a question of *interdependence*, sensed as a *system determining* relationships in the contemporary world, in its economic, cultural, political and religious elements, and accepted as a *moral category*. When interdependence becomes recognized in this way, the correlative response as a moral and social attitude, as a "virtue," is *solidarity*. This then is not a feeling of vague compassion or shallow distress at the misfortunes of so many people both near and far. On the contrary, it is a *firm and persevering determination* to commit oneself to the *common good*; that is to say to the good of all and each individual, because we are *all* really responsible for *all.* (SRS 38)

Solidarity is the only response to interdependence that allows for authentic development. The desire for power or profit cannot afford true development. The center of this social ethic is always the human person and, by virtue of the human person, humanity itself. Interdependence as a moral category is what leads to understanding solidarity as a duty. The reality of interdependence elicits a response among human persons, who are always individuals in communities, of the personhood of others. Solidarity is a response to interdependence with a deep and abiding commitment to the equality, mutuality, and dignity of every member of the human family. This growing recognition of our human dignity and that of others begins with a natural inclination, an attitude, which for John Paul II can be developed into the virtue of solidarity; however, he does not specify what the virtue of solidarity is or entails. The closest examination of this is found in his statements on living authentic solidarity.

For solidarity to be authentic requires that it pervade every level of human society. Solidarity is not something that only applies to the poor or oppressed. True solidarity involves a mutual recognition of the equal personhood of all. An attitude of solidarity of the workers or poor among themselves and of the rich and powerful among themselves is not sufficient. "The exercise of solidarity *within each society* is valid when its members recognize one another as persons. Those who are more influential, because they have a greater share of goods and common services, should feel responsible for the weaker and be ready to share with them all they possess" (SRS 39). Living in solidarity on the part of the rich, on the part of those who have participation, requires that they act in accordance with the common good, which ultimately requires the relinquishing of power and control. That is, those in power are required, by solidarity, not only to share materially with the rest of the community but to allow those on the margins to participate. This must include redistribution of power in favor of the authentic participation by all. Furthermore, "interdependence must be transformed into solidarity, based upon the principle that the goods of creation are meant for all. That which human industry produces through the processing of raw materials, with the contribution of work, must serve equally for the good of all" (SRS 39). Living in solidarity cannot be relegated to the rich *giving* to the poor. It is a dynamic concept that involves mutual responsibility. Just as the rich and powerful are required to recognize the participation of the weaker, "those who are weaker, for their part, in the same spirit of solidarity, should not adopt a purely *passive* attitude or one that is *destructive* of the social fabric, but, while claiming their legitimate rights, should do what they can for the good of all" (SRS 39). This is a moral obligation to oppose injustice and through this opposition to demand participation in community. In doing so, they are not acting against the common good but for the good of all.

Thus, John Paul II offers his most extensive and most forceful defense of solidarity as the path to peace and development. Against structures of sin, exploitation, and oppression, "the solidarity which we propose is the *path to peace and at the same time to development.* For world peace is inconceivable unless the world's leaders come to recognize that interdependence in itself demands the abandonment of the politics of blocs, the sacrifice of all forms of economic, military or political imperialism, and the transformation of mutual distrust into *collaboration.* This is precisely the *act proper* to solidarity among individuals and nations" (SRS 39). Where his predecessors used solidarity as a substitute for love and development as the new name for peace, John Paul II argues that the path to peace is solidarity. True community and living a truly human life depends on solidarity.

Creation of the human person and the universal destination of goods are repeatedly offered as the foundation for solidarity. This is because "solidarity helps us to see the 'other'—whether as a *person, people* or *nation*—not just as some kind of instrument, with a work capacity and physical strength to be exploited at low cost and then discarded when no longer useful, but as our 'neighbor,' a 'helper' (cf Gen. 2:18-20), to be made a sharer, on par with ourselves, in the banquet of life to which all are equally invited by God" (SRS 39). According to Kevin Doran, "When the solidarity of a person is described as an attitude, it has a significance which has to do primarily with its outward direction towards other persons, their needs, and the structures of society within which they are called to be and to act."[34] The attitude of solidarity, then, is the recognition in the face of interdependence of our common humanity and the importance of the common good: "The attitude aids one to have constant disposition of responsibility and relationship in the community not only because one is a member of the community, but because one is always aware and concerned with the common good."[35] In its many dimensions, solidarity is emerging as the way to live a truly human life. We become more fully human, in our individual lives and in community, through this solidarity.

Solidarity, then, is as much an integral aspect of the human person as human rights. Theologically, it is integral to how we understand the human person as *imago dei* and as related to our understanding of the Trinity. In his section on solidarity as a *Christian virtue*, John Paul II states, "One's neighbor is then not only a human being with his own rights and a fundamental equality with everyone else; but becomes the *living image* of God the father, redeemed by the blood of Jesus Christ and placed under the permanent action of the Holy Spirit" (SRS 40). John Paul II further expands on this theological importance of understanding solidarity within the context of the Trinity and *imago dei* through the relationship between solidarity and communion. "Beyond human and natural bonds, already so close and strong, there is discerned in the light of *faith* a new model of the *unity* of the human race, which ultimately inspires our *solidarity*. This supreme *model of unity*, which is a reflection of the intimate life for God; one God in three persons is what we Christians mean by the word

34. Kevin P. Doran, *Solidarity: A Synthesis of Personalism and Communalism in the Thought of Karol Wojtyla / Pope John Paul II* (New York: Peter Lang, 1996), 191.

35. Marie Vianney Bilgrien, SSND, *Solidarity: A Principle, an Attitude, a Duty or the Virtue for an Independent World?* (New York: Peter Lang, 1999), 48.

communion" (SRS 40). What is at stake is the very *dignity of the human person*, understood as "the indestructible image of God the creator, which is *identical in each one of us*" (SRS 47). Therefore, the only way to overcome structures of sin and have authentic development both nationally and internationally is through solidarity. However, the connection between solidarity and the *imago dei* goes beyond seeing our neighbor as an image of God; it has to be based also on our faith in the Trinity. Not only are we modeling human solidarity on the communion of the Trinity, but in solidarity we see the image of the living God, the Trinitarian God—one God in three persons. This connection between solidarity and the *imago dei* is not developed further in John Paul II but is integral to understanding the connection between solidarity and human rights.

In his 1991 encyclical, *Centesimus Annus* (*On the Hundredth Year*), John Paul II reflects back on one hundred years of Catholic social teaching and commemorates the fall of communism in Eastern Europe. In doing so, he firmly argues for the centrality of human rights and continues to define solidarity in broad but vague terms, grounding all in the specifics of theological or philosophical anthropology. Both the reflections back to *Rerum Novarum* and the fall of the Berlin Wall are springboards to reaffirming the importance of the rights of the person, now understood as universal human rights. In this holistic view of humanity as persons in community the fundamental error of socialism's anthropology can be found, "A person who is deprived of something he can call 'his own,' and of the possibility of earning a living through his own initiative, comes to depend on the social machine and on those who control it. This makes it much more difficult for him to recognize his dignity as a person, and hinders progress towards the building up of an authentic human community" (CA 13). If one does not have an authentic view of the person, then one cannot have an authentically human personal or social ethics.

On the subject of human rights, *Centesimus Annus* speaks more descriptively than John Paul II's earlier encyclicals. Instead of focusing on the specific rights and duties defined earlier, this document focuses on actual instances of promoting human rights and the effect of human rights in the historical events of 1989 (CA 22). However, John Paul II does focus on the particular role of the state in protecting the conditions of workers. With reference to *Rerum Novarum* (*On the Condition of Workers*), the pope does not simply acquiesce to capitalism, as is evident in sections on freedom (CA 17, 25) and the failures of the market (CA 34). He explains that "development must not be understood solely in economic terms, but in a way that is fully human" (CA 29). Furthering his arguments for the necessity of solidarity, he moves from a focus on solidarity as a Christian virtue to the language of *the principle of solidarity*. This principle, as applied to states, requires that they defend the weak and poor "by placing certain limits on the autonomy of the parties who determine working conditions and by ensuring in every case the necessary minimum support for the unemployment worker" (CA 15). Given the encyclical's focus on workers and the state, its use of solidarity references the duties imposed by solidarity.

Focus on Charity: Human Rights and Solidarity in Benedict XVI

A philosopher and ethicist's voice permeates John Paul II's trilogy of social encyclicals. Human rights and solidarity are developed with key attention to the dignity of the human person, interpreted through the lens of Thomistic personalism and phenomenology. With the election of Joseph Ratzinger, this emphasis shifted to systematic theology and *caritas* as hermeneutical principle. In 2006, Pope Benedict XVI released his first encyclical, *Deus Caritas Est* (*God Is Love*), a theological and pastoral encyclical focused on reclaiming the rich Christian theological tradition on *caritas*. An encyclical addressed internally to the church, *Deus Caritas Est* provides an extended theological meditation on the nature of love and Christian charity primarily in dialogue with secular philosophy. Similar to John Paul II, whose theological and pastoral encyclical *Redemptor Hominis* provided a theological context for the theological ethics found in *Laborem Exercens*, Pope Benedict XVI uses the theological focus on *caritas* as a building block for his first social encyclical, *Caritas in Veritate* (*Charity in Truth*). Commemorating the fortieth anniversary of *Populorum Progressio* and responding to the global financial crisis, *Caritas in Veritate* offers further development of human rights and solidarity through the theological lens of *caritas*. Benedict XVI's contribution to Catholic social teaching, *Caritas in Veritate* enhances the theological foundation for solidarity through vocation and the principle of gratuitousness and expands solidarity through the concept of intergenerational justice. Yet, ambiguities concerning the relationship between human rights and the virtue of solidarity remain.

While it is not a social encyclical, *Deus Caritas Est* clearly establishes *caritas* as a controlling concept for Benedict XVI's emerging contribution to Catholic social teaching. God is love. This at first glance appears quite obvious, and yet in choosing this as his starting point, Benedict's explicit goal is to complicate, correct, and enrich the Christian use of the word *love*. Love is a word with many meanings and is "frequently used and misused" (DCE 2); however, Christian love or *caritas* presents itself simultaneously as gift and demand, uniting love of God and love of neighbor. In brief, this recovery of the rich Christian understanding of *caritas* as gift and task, the "unbreakable bond between love of God and love of neighbor" (DCE 16), and the universalizing of *neighbor* provide a theological context for the development of human rights and solidarity found within *Caritas in Veritate*.[36]

Throughout the *Deus Caritas Est*, Benedict XVI emphasizes that "love can only be 'commanded' because it has first been given" (DCE14). The biblical affirmations that *God is love* are primarily statements that the love of God is first and is offered to us as gift. Through creation and covenant, God offers love as gift, and we are called and commanded to respond to it. For Benedict, this is at the heart of the Christian understanding of *eros* and *agape* as well as the distinctive ethical demand within Christian charity. What is charity? Common usage has reduced *caritas*, or charity, to the practice of almsgiving. While almsgiving is one aspect of practicing charity, reducing charity in this way eclipses the heart of the biblical understanding of the love of God as well as the rich Christian theological tradition in which charity is not simply a set of practices but also a virtue and friendship with God.[37] At the heart of this theological meditation is the insistence that *caritas* is fundamentally a relationship of love initiated by God to which we are called to respond. This understanding of the role of gift in the love of God provides the theological foundation for the emphasis on *gratuitousness* Benedict later develops in *Caritas in Veritate*.

36. The final section of *Deus Caritas Est* offers a reflection on the relationship between charity and justice, in particular the role of justice in politics and the social ordering of the state. This section has created significant debate concerning the role of the church, religious groups, and the laity in the pursuit of justice and a just social order. As this is not a social encyclical and is only being examined here to provide theological context for *Caritas in Veritate*, it is not examined in this book. However, extensive interpretations and debate concerning the meaning of the final section of *Deus Caritas Est* can be found in Avery Dulles, SJ, "The Indirect Mission of the Church to Politics," *Villanova Law Review* 52, no. 2 (2007): 241–52; Samuel Gregg "Deus Caritas Est: The Social Message of the Pope," *Economic Affairs* 26, 2 (2006) p. 55-59.; Charles M. Murphy, "Charity, not Justice, as Constitutive of the Church's Mission," *Theological Studies* 68 (2007): 274–86; and Thomas Massaro, SJ, "Don't Forget Justice," *America Magazine*, March 13, 2006, http://www.americamagazine.org/content/article.cfm?article_id=4669.

37. For more on this see Thomas Aquinas, *Summa Theologiae*, trans. Fathers of the English Dominican Province (Allen, TX: Christian Classics, 1991); Gerard Gilleman, SJ, *The Primacy of Charity in Moral Theology* (Westminster, MD: Newman Press, 1959); Meghan J. Clark, "The Complex but Necessary Union of Charity and Justice: Insights from the Vincentian Tradition for Contemporary Catholic Social Teaching," *Vincentian Heritage Journal* 31, no. 2 (2012): 25–39; and Meghan J. Clark, "Love of God and Neighbor: Living Charity in Aquinas' Ethics," *New Blackfriars* 92, no. 1040 (July 2011): 415–30.

What then is the model of *caritas?* How does the Christian model his or her response to the love of God? The answer is provided in the person of Jesus Christ who is the incarnate love of God (DCE 12) and who concretely reveals the "unbreakable bond between love of God and love of neighbor" (DCE 16). Benedict XVI explains, "Union with Christ is also union with all those to whom he gives himself. I cannot possess Christ just for myself; I can belong to him only in union with all who have become or will become his own. Communion draws me out of myself towards him and thus towards unity with all Christians. We become 'one body,' completely joined in a single existence. Love of God and love of neighbor are now truly united: God incarnate draws all to himself" (DCE 14). In accordance with this, love of neighbor is the concrete responsibility of each and every Christian as well as the responsibility of the church as a local and global entity. "As a community, the Church must practice love. Love thus needs to be organized if it is to be an ordered service to the community" (DCE 20). The clearest model of this was presented in Acts 2:44-45; "within the community of believers there can be no room for a poverty that denies anyone what is needed for a dignified life" (DCE 20). *Caritas* as love of God and neighbor, then, is at the very heart of the mission and identity of the Christian community.

This union with Christ as union with the community is important for expanding the theological significance of solidarity; however, it is imperative to address the identity of *neighbor.* Christians are called to be a community of believers in which they are required to organize love of neighbor so as to provide the conditions (material and spiritual) of a dignified life. However, while the purpose of this encyclical is an internal one, the practice of *caritas* within the community of believers cannot be limited to the Christian community. In the unity of love of God and love of neighbor, one cannot understand love of neighbor as an internal command limited to the Christian community. An essential aspect of this encounter with the incarnate love of God, in which Benedict XVI presents the perfect union between love of God and love of neighbor, is that the concept of neighbor is universalized. Through exposition of the parable of the good Samaritan and the last judgment in Matthew 25, he makes clear, "Anyone who needs me, and whom I can help is my neighbor. The concept of 'neighbor' is now universalized, it remains concrete" (DCE 15). Love of neighbor is not abstract, cannot be fulfilled simply through internal practices directed at the Christian community, and places a concrete demand upon the believer.

At the heart of Benedict's exposition of *Deus Caritas Est*, then, is the pragmatic call to solidarity of all with all; "love of God and love of neighbor have become one: in the least of the brethren we find Jesus himself, and in Jesus we find God" (DCE 15), a framework that will be the foundation for *Caritas in Veritate*. For Benedict XVI, "This dynamic of charity received and given is what gives rise to the Church's social teaching, which is *caritas in veritate in re sociali*: the proclamation of the truth of Christ's love in society" (CV 5). Thus, he argues that *caritas* "gives real substance to the personal relationship with God and with neighbor; it is the principle not only of micro-relationships (with friends, family members or within small groups) but also of macro-relationships (social, economic, and political ones)" (CV2). Thus, *Caritas in Veritate* (*Charity in Truth*) enters into conversation with multiple dialogue partners commemorating the fortieth anniversary of *Populorum Progressio* and responding to a devastating global financial crisis. In keeping with its predecessors, human rights and solidarity play crucial roles in both its theological vision and ethical evaluations.

Where *Deus Caritas Est* created significant controversy for its narrowed understanding of the relationship between charity and justice, *Caritas in Veritate* brings justice back into focus and clarifies its relationship to charity. Leaving little room for confusion, Benedict XVI states, "I cannot 'give' what is mine to the other, without first giving him what pertains to him in justice. If we love others with charity, then first of all we are just towards them" (CV 6). I cannot meet the demands of *caritas* if I do not first meet the requirements of justice; it is a necessary prerequisite for the practice of *caritas*. Thus, we cannot effectively love our neighbor if justice is not present. To provide the theological foundation for his approach, Benedict XVI emphasizes the role of *vocation* in integral human development. Cautioning against placing too much faith in institutions, he argues, "Integral human development is primarily a *vocation* and therefore it involves a free assumption of responsibility in solidarity on the part of everyone" (CV 11). While it may appear as if Benedict were weighing in on debates concerning the role of institutions compared to individual responsibility, this interpretation is countered by his insistence on "the institutional path—we might call it the political path—of charity, no less excellent and effective than the kind of charity which encounters the neighbor directly" (CV 7).[38] There is a deeper theology here that is not properly understood within the philosophical and political debate about individuals and structures. For Benedict XVI and Catholic social teaching, *vocation* is a relational category that begins with the transcendent vision of the human person, created

38. This narrow interpretation of *Caritas in Veritate* being rejected here is found in George Weigel's "Caritas in Veritate in Red and Gold," *National Review*, July 7, 2009, http://www.nationalreview.com/articles/227839/i-caritas-veritate-i-gold-and-red/george-weigel.

in the image of God, in relationship to God, and responsible to recognize her neighbor as in the image of God. Thus, "a vocation is a call that requires a free and responsible answer. Integral human development presupposes the responsible freedom of the individual and of peoples: no structure can guarantee this development over and above human responsibility" (CV 17). Pragmatically, development cannot happen without just structures. This was an important insight of Paul VI in *Populorum Progressio*; however, Benedict is arguing that without the response to God and neighbor on behalf of individuals and peoples, development will not be integral or grounded in solidarity. The crucial point here is not individual freedom but the vocation of *peoples*. The vocation of development requires the free and responsible freedom *of peoples*. In addition, from this understanding of development as vocation, *charity in truth* builds community because "the human being is made for gift, which expresses and makes present his transcendent dimension" as an expression of fraternity (CV 34). On the one hand, emphasizing the free assumption of responsibility by persons, Benedict notes that "solidarity is first and foremost a sense of responsibility of everyone with regard to everyone, it cannot therefore be merely relegated to the state" (CV 38). On the other hand, this free assumption of responsibility is demanded not only of individuals but of peoples. Instead of moving from the community to the individual, the vocation of *peoples* for development in solidarity firmly establishes that development is *our* vocation.

Using the *economic reality* exposed by the global financial crisis, Benedict links vocation with the *principle of gratuitousness* as foundational for solidarity (CV 36). At present, the global situation is marked by a weakening of and attack on unions, which are the "traditional networks of solidarity" (CV 25), as well as a lessening of the basic mutual trust needed within economic markets for regular economic function (CV 35). Thus, "in the global era, economic activity cannot prescind from gratuitousness, which fosters and disseminates solidarity and responsibility for justice and the common good among the different economic players" (CV 38). Through its treatment of the economic sphere, *Caritas in Veritate* uses solidarity in three distinct ways. First, an attitude of solidarity is connected to the basic level of mutual trust needed for the basic function of economic markets (CV 35). Second, using the theology of vocation, Benedict interprets solidarity through a strongly relational theological anthropology—the unity of the one human family as created in the image of God, as neighbors. While it remains somewhat vague, the principle of gratuitousness is central to Benedict's conception of the human family. So much so that he states, "Today it is clear that without gratuitousness, there can be no justice in the first place" (CV 38), arguing that "both the market and politics need individuals who are open to reciprocal gift" (CV 39). Once again, *Caritas in Veritate* builds its vision of justice and solidarity in development on the theology of vocation. And third, through the lens of vocation and *gratuitousness*, solidarity is a profound duty for all human persons and communities.

Linking human rights and solidarity through duties, Benedict highlights the problem of *food insecurity* and basic human rights, stating, "The right to food, like the right to water, has an important place within the pursuit of other rights, beginning with the fundamental right to life. It is therefore necessary to cultivate a public conscience that considers *food and access to water as universal rights of all human beings without distinction or discrimination*" (CV 27). When the understanding of human rights is divorced from a sense of duty, those rights that are most basic and should have the easiest agreement fall to the wayside.

> The link consists in this: individual rights, when detached from a framework of duties which grants them their full meaning, can run wild, leading to an escalation of demands which is effectively unlimited and indiscriminate. An over emphasis on rights leads to a disregard for duties. Duties set a limit on the rights because they point to the anthropological and ethical framework of which rights are a part, in this way ensuring that they do not become license. Duties thereby reinforce rights and call for their defense and promotion as a task to be undertaken in service of the common good. (CV 43)

Benedict XVI is attempting simultaneously to hold up the centrality of basic human rights, in particular food security and access to clean, safe drinking water; to argue against the *right to excess* among developed nations; and to forward the duty of all individuals and peoples as members of the human family.[39] Aside from reiterating the duties corresponding to human rights and focusing this around the theology of vocation, *Caritas in Veritate* does not significantly develop or add to the established Catholic social teaching on human rights. The primary contribution is found in its bringing the theology of vocation (and by extension, *gratuitousness*) to the forefront of understanding the corresponding duties associated with human rights.

With regard to solidarity, *Caritas in Veritate*'s significant contribution to Catholic social teaching is found within its focus not on *caritas* but on vocation.

---

39. Similarly, the universal responsibility for the environment and creation is another example used in *Caritas in Veritate* to demonstrate the vocation of humanity for human rights and solidarity (CV 43–52).

Despite its explicit use of *Populorum Progressio* and *Sollicitudo Rei Socialis*, there is not significant treatment of solidarity as a virtue or of concrete practices of solidarity. *Caritas in Veritate* remains much more on the theoretical level, seeking to reframe the discussion anthropologically on the one human family and the human vocation (in response to God and neighbor). In doing so, solidarity is largely treated as a duty and as something lacking in the global financial structure. This anthropological focus is evident in Benedict XVI's argument for the relationship between solidarity and subsidiarity, for intergenerational justice and solidarity with future generations. Using concern for environmental integrity and sustainability, Benedict states, "Consequently, projects for integral human development cannot ignore coming generations, but need to be marked by solidarity and *intergenerational justice*, while taking into account a variety of contexts: ecological, juridical, economic, political, and cultural" (CV 48). Integral human development as a vocation of individuals and of peoples extends to future generations, and so we must strive to foster solidarity with future generations. Thus, "the theme of development can be identified with the inclusion-in-relation of all individuals and peoples within the one community of the human family, built in solidarity on the basis of fundamental values of justice and peace. This perspective is illuminated in a striking way by the relationship between the Persons in the Trinity within the one divine Substance" (CV 54). Ultimately, this theological retrieval of *caritas* and emphasis on vocation is a refocusing of the question of solidarity and development on humanity as created in the image and likeness of God—the dignity of the human person and the dignity of the one human family. Therefore, it is fitting that *Caritas in Veritate* ends with a call for scholars, including theologians, to engage in "*a deeper critical evaluation of the category of relation . . .* if man's transcendent dignity is to be properly understood" (CV 53).

CONCLUSION

Beginning with John XXIII and Paul VI, Catholic social teaching offers a clear and succinct approach to human rights. Where later encyclicals often seek to correct and update earlier social teaching in the area of human rights, the writings of both John Paul II and Benedict XVI deepen and expand aspects of human rights teaching.[40] The meaning of solidarity, however, is not offered in a clear and comprehensive way. From Paul VI through Benedict XVI, solidarity is referred to as an attitude, a duty, a virtue, and a principle. Each

---

40. For example, *Quadragesimo Anno* contains a tempering of *Rerum Novarum's* statements on private property.

focus illuminates a different important aspect of solidarity, yet, taken as a whole, this allows solidarity to remain ambiguous. Solidarity is both an integral theme in Catholic social teaching and one whose meaning is difficult to pin down. A clear example of this is found in *Centesimus Annus*. Highlighting continuity, John Paul II states:

> In this way what we nowadays call the principle of solidarity, the validity of which both in the internal order of each nation and in the international I have discussed in the encyclical *Sollicitudo Rei Socialis*, is clearly seen to be one of the fundamental principles of the Christian view of social and political organization. This principle is frequently stated by Pope Leo XIII, who uses the term *friendship*, a concept already found in Greek philosophy. Pius XI refers to it with the equally meaningful term *social charity*. Pope Paul VI, expanding the concept to cover the many modern aspects of the social question speaks of a *civilization of love*. (CA 10)

Friendship, social charity, and love all involve social relationships and thus all have something in common with solidarity. However, is it really accurate to state that they are all different words for the same thing? Not quite. While they all appear to be building to solidarity, solidarity goes beyond these earlier terms and cannot be contained by any one of them.

The clearest definition of solidarity comes in *Sollicitudo Rei Socialis*'s identification of solidarity as a moral category: "When interdependence becomes recognized in this way, the correlative response as a moral and social attitude, as a 'virtue,' is solidarity. This then is not a feeling of vague compassion or shallow distress at the misfortunes of so many people, both near and far. On the contrary, it is a firm and persevering determination to commit oneself to the common good; that is to say to the good of all and of each individual, because we are all really responsible for all" (SRS 38). Like human rights, solidarity is a moral category predicated on mutuality. Only through the mutual respect for the personhood of each and every human person can human rights or solidarity be accomplished. Interdependence is a historical reality, whether recognized or not. It is a reality that applies not only to humanity, but to the entire created world. This can, however, be transformed into solidarity through attitude, duty, virtue, and principle. In the end, solidarity as a virtue may be the most comprehensive way to understand it, as the concept of virtue includes the others. In studying the use of solidarity in Catholic social teaching, Marie Vianney Bilgrien, SSND, admits that, despite the fact that John Paul

II calls solidarity a virtue, he does not write extensively on what that means, and so in developing her own understanding of solidarity, she relies largely on other theoretical writings on the virtue of solidarity, for example the work of Marciano Vidal. After an extensive study of the word and concept of solidarity, Bilgrien offers seven important elements of solidarity:

> 1. Interdependence is a fact and solidarity emerged through the consciousness of that actuality.
> 2. Solidarity is based on the reality of our human equality and dignity.
> 3. Solidarity works for the common good of all.
> 4. Solidarity must be practiced with an awareness of the poor.
> 5. Solidarity must be a firm and persevering determination.
> 6. Solidarity is not just a virtue of individual persons, but also of groups and nations.
> 7. Compassion, empathy, and mercy move solidarity into action and help sustain the disposition.[41]

Her seven points are helpful in thinking about solidarity and point out key elements that must be present. Yet, they do not remove the ambiguity of what is required to apply solidarity. Simply calling it a virtue is not sufficient to pin down what we mean by calling solidarity a cornerstone of Catholic social ethics. If solidarity is a virtue, what are its principles? How do we make habitual the practices of solidarity? Answering these questions requires looking at the human person and the deeply social nature of both communities and our personal freedom and agency. Theologically, this points to the connection between solidarity and seeing each person as created in the image and likeness of God. However, the implication of our creation in the image of God goes deeper than individuals. It is in solidarity that the human family images the living God, the Trinity, which is a connection indicated by Benedict XVI's emphasis on God and the theological richness of charity.

Where human rights are concerned, we have a set of principles grounded in the dignity of the human person. They have been well established and delineated, even granting that many of them continue to need deeper reflection and much greater implementation. The grounding for solidarity, like that of human rights, is in the human person. Just as Catholic social teaching has attempted to develop human rights in an inclusive way, offering an understanding of the community and duties that go along with these rights, so too solidarity is based on the dignity of the human person, a free, rational,

41. Bilgrien, *Solidarity*, 105–6.

and social being created in the image and likeness of God. Modern Catholic social teaching clearly argues that an authentic moral view of the human person must include both human rights and solidarity. In order to understand the connection between human rights and solidarity, and to gain a clearer exposition of solidarity, one must turn to the human person.

Anthropological Foundations for Human Rights and Solidarity

"We must reappropriate the true meaning of freedom, which is not an intoxication with total autonomy, but a response to the call of being, beginning with our own personal being."
Pope Benedict XVI, *Caritas in Veritate* 70

"We are one human family. By simply being born into this world, we are of one inheritance and one stock with every other human being. This oneness expresses itself in all the richness and diversity of the human family: in different races, cultures, languages and histories. And we are called to recognize the basic solidarity of the human family as the fundamental condition of our life together on this earth."
Pope John Paul II, World Day of Peace Message (1987)

When the Universal Declaration of Human Rights was drafted and approved, Jacques Maritain and others noted that there was remarkable consensus concerning the content of the document, provided that no one asked *why*. In 1948, the document was approved and the *age of human rights* began in international affairs. Catholic social encyclicals are often similarly critiqued for not providing extensive arguments for their statements. Encyclicals do not provide the philosophical and theological foundations or arguments, mainly because of the limits of the genre. It is not what encyclicals do—they are not theological or philosophical treatises. However, in the twenty-first century one thing is now clear: a full appreciation of either the Universal Declaration or Catholic social doctrine requires grappling with those foundations and being able to argue *why*. As we contend with a deeply divided world with violence, poverty, inequality, and environmental degradation, the future of human rights and Catholic social doctrine requires greater attention to the foundational question: Why? For Christian theology, this is an anthropological question. The why of human rights and solidarity becomes a question of who: Who is the human person? Who are we? Implementing human rights and developing an ethics of solidarity involve investigating the role of the individual and the community, the human person and humanity as a whole. In order to ground the necessary and intimate connection between human rights and solidarity, I offer a philosophical and theological anthropology of a community of equal human persons. Through our understanding of human freedom and the human person as created *imago dei*, human rights and solidarity both flow necessarily from what it means to be human. Philosophically, freedom and rights must be understood as socially embedded in communities. In order to examine that foundation, I turn to Charles Taylor's argument for situated freedom, a modern social imaginary and as members, our obligation to belong. Theologically, the starting point for both human rights and solidarity is the human person as created *imago dei*. For Christians, to be in the image and likeness of God must be understood as *imago trinitatis*. How is it we are created in the image and likeness of the Trinity? Through contemporary feminist Trinitarian theology, specifically that of Elizabeth Johnson, CSJ, and Catherine LaCugna, the principles of equality, mutuality, and reciprocity emerge as practical criteria to be applied to the human person and community. Within the theological and philosophical anthropology presented, an intimate and unbreakable link between your dignity and my own emerges and, with it, a profound ethical obligation for both human rights and solidarity.

THE SOCIAL NATURE OF THE HUMAN AGENT AND THE OBLIGATION TO BELONG

The starting point for both human rights and solidarity is the human person. Human beings are social animals, and interdependence is an observable reality. However, when *Populorum Progressio* categorizes interdependence as a normative and ethical category, Pope Paul VI is making a much stronger claim about the sociality of human beings than can be found in mainstream liberal philosophy. What then is the philosophy of the human person linking human rights and solidarity? Canadian philosopher Charles Taylor develops a philosophical anthropology that takes seriously the human person as both a bearer of rights and a member of community. Through his attention to the modern moral order, the self, and the obligation to belong, a rich and multifaceted philosophical anthropology emerges that grounds both human rights and solidarity in the human person.

GROUNDING THE SELF IN THE MODERN SOCIAL IMAGINARY

"I am arguing that the free individual of the West is only what he is by virtue of the whole society and civilization which brought him to be and which nourishes him."
Charles Taylor[1]

"Self-knowledge is only possible when we share in greater memory."
Pope Francis, Lumen Fidei 38

Catholic social thought emphasizes human freedom and self-knowledge but only within a *greater memory* constantly in relationships with the community as well as both previous and future generations. Known for his attention to modernity, the self, and the protection of distinctive communal identities, Charles Taylor reframes the discussion beginning with the "modern social imaginary" instead of the individual or a particular theory.[2] Both normative and factual, the social imaginary "incorporates a sense of the normal expectations that we have of each other; the common understanding which enables us to carry out the collective practices which make up our social life."[3] A new social imaginary is more than an evaluation of particular practices, according to Taylor; it is also accompanied by "(i) new forms of narrativity and (ii) new understandings of social bonds and relations."[4] Through attention to narrative identity, freedom, and the modern social imaginary, a consistent and

---

1. Charles Taylor, "Atomism," Pilosophical Papers, vol.2: Philosophy and the Human Sciences (Cambridge: Cambridge University Press, 1985), 206.

2. Where social theory is often espoused only by the few, Taylor is trying to address a broader social reality. For this reason, he turns to a social imaginary that includes "the ways people imagine their social existence, how they fit together with others, and how things go on between them and their fellows, their expectations that are normally met and the deeper normative notions and image that underlie these expectations." While ordinary people rarely understand and express their social situation on the level of theory, "humans operated with a social imaginary well before they ever got into the business of theorizing about themselves." However, social theory is not irrelevant; it influences and develops the social imaginary as the modern social imaginary clearly illustrates. Charles Taylor, *Modern Social Imaginaries* (Durham, NC: Duke University Press, 2004), 23, 26.

3. Charles Taylor, *A Secular Age* (Cambridge, MA: Harvard University Press, 2009), 172.

4. Charles Taylor, *Sources of the Self: The Making of Modern Identity* (Cambridge: Cambridge University Press, 1992), 105.

philosophically rigorous approach to the human person emerges as characterized both by human rights and the challenge of solidarity. Thus, from Taylor's anthropological conclusion that "selfhood and the good, or in another way, selfhood and morality, turn out to be inextricably intertwined themes," the inextricably intertwined themes of human rights and solidarity come into focus.[5]

A basic feature of human existence is that "our condition can never be exhausted for us by what we *are*, because we are always changing and *becoming*. It is only slowly that we grow through infancy and childhood to be autonomous agents who have something like our own place relative to the good. . . . So the issue for us has to be not only where we *are* but where we're *going*."[6] We do not, however, develop a life plan or make qualitative distinctions alone or in a vacuum. They require a social matrix. "As organisms, we are separable from society . . . but as humans this separation is unthinkable"; a human person is always in relation to others.[7] This is central to Catholic social teaching's reflection on both interdependence and globalization. By definition, a person is both subject and respondent, a being to whom a question can be asked and who can respond. The very question *who* places "someone as a potential interlocutor in a society of interlocutors."[8]

The clearest and most common illustration of this is language: "A language only exists and is maintained within a language community. And this indicates another crucial feature of a self. One is a self only among other selves. A self can never be described without reference to those who surround it."[9] In a manner similar to that of Pope John Paul II's personalism, the self here is built upon a conception of the person as both subject and respondent, for which language and dialogue are crucial examples. Formally, "we are always socially embedded; we learn our identities in dialogue, by being inducted into

5. Ibid, 3.

6. Ibid., 47. Cf. also "The notion of identity refers us to certain evaluations which are essential because they are the indispensable horizon or foundation out of which we reflect and evaluate as persons. . . . The subject of radical choice is another avatar of that recurrent figure which our civilization aspires to realize, the disembodied ego, the subject who can objectify all being, including his own, and choose in radical freedom. But this promised total self-possession would in fact be the most total self loss" (35). To be a self, in Taylor's strong sense, is to evaluate one's constitutive good and "a constitutive good is basic to being responsible for ourselves." William Schweiker, "The Good and Moral Identity: A Theological Ethical Response to Charles Taylor's Sources of the Self," *Journal of Religion* 72, no. 4 (1992): 562.

7. Charles Taylor, introduction to *Philosophical Papers*, vol. 2: *Philosophy and the Human Sciences* (Cambridge: Cambridge University Press, 1985), 3.

8. Taylor, *Sources of the Self*, 29.

9. Ibid, 35.

a certain language."[10] In order to speak and communicate, an individual must learn a particular language, its grammatical structure, its vocabulary, and so on. Learning the rules of a language, however, does not prevent one from being creative, inventing new ideas, expressions, and the like. Thus, language provides a clear example of the necessary mutuality between the individual and community and serves as a reminder that individuality is not lost but maintained through that community. In *Common Good and Christian Ethics*, David Hollenbach explains, "The shared good of a language is not merely an instrument that individuals use to communicate; it is constitutive of speech itself. . . . The common and the individual mutually interpenetrate and mutually determine each other."[11] The analogy illustrates that the moral freedom of the modern individual is not diminished by being socially embedded but instead this freedom substantively exists because of it. The social matrix provides the conditions of possibility for our agency and life plans to be developed and executed. These life plans are not neutral or culture free.[12]

The focus here is not on an isolated individual or a confining culture but on *narrative identity* as foundational for our understanding of the human person.[13] In particular, the fundamental question *who am I* is a question of a narrative identity involving our past, present, and future. Answering the question requires an understanding of where one stands in relation to the *web of interlocutors* briefly mentioned above. For Taylor, "My identity is defined by the commitments and identifications which provide the frame or horizon within which I can try to determine from case to case what is good, or valuable, or what ought to be done, or what I endorse or oppose. In other words, it is the horizon within which I am capable of taking a stand."[14] This narrative identity involves our standing within a horizon of the good and our making strong evaluations. While these evaluations may change, there is a trajectory through

10. Taylor, *Modern Social Imaginaries*, 65.

11. David Hollenbach, *Common Good and Christian Ethics* (Cambridge: Cambridge University Press, 2002), 74.

12. Another example would be the concepts of honor or humiliation. Taylor explains, "We understand the inclination to hide what is humiliating, only through understanding what is humiliating. Someone who had no grasp of a culture's sense of shame would never know what constituted successful case of hiding . . . let alone why they want to do it." Charles Taylor, "The Concept of a Person," in *Philosophical Papers*, vol. 1: *Human Agency and Language* (Cambridge: Cambridge University Press, 1985), 108.

13. Taylor, *Sources of the Self*, 50.

14. Ibid., 27. Without this horizon, one finds oneself in an *identity crisis*, "an acute form of disorientation, which people often express in terms of not knowing who they are, but which can also be seen as a radical uncertainty of where they stand. They lack a frame or horizon within which things can take on a stable significance, within which some life possibilities can be seen as good or meaningful" (27).

time. "The various moments in a life, in relation to which we understand who we are, have a *direction.* The fact that the story I am living projects me into a future, to a self I am not yet, but which must be of concern, gives my life, indeed all human life, the character of a 'quest.'"[15] Thus, an orientation to the good and narrative identity are, for Taylor, "inescapable structural requirements of human agency."[16] Instead of establishing selfhood apart from the social matrix, the modern self and its narrative identity are always embedded in this modern world of freedom, equality, and human rights. Similarly, in *Lumen Fidei* Pope Francis highlights that "self-knowledge is only possible when we share in greater memory" (LF 38).

Where this background of a social imaginary begins and ends is vague.[17] Through human history, a number of social imaginaries existed before the current *modern social imaginary.* The modern social imaginary emerges after the Enlightenment and, as understood by Taylor, provides the foundation for both universal human rights and solidarity. What is special or different about the modern social imaginary? The premodern social imaginary was marked by a hierarchical order deeply embedded in an enchanted world in which the self existed in a natural, divinely instituted moral order. The modern social imaginary, on the other hand, begins with the anthropological claim of natural law that "human beings are rational, sociable agents who are meant to collaborate in peace to their mutual benefit," and thus "rights can now be seriously pleaded against power."[18] A vision of persons as self-interpreting, modern, free, and embedded agents with an obligation to belong arises. Through the many redactions in the last four hundred years, four distinct characteristics of the modern moral order develop.[19] First, it is an order between individuals freed from the previous hierarchical orders. Its "benefits (2) crucially include life and the means to live, however securing these relates to the practice of virtue; it is meant (3) to secure freedom and easily finds expression in terms of rights. To these we can add a fourth point: (4) these rights, this freedom, this mutual benefit is to be secured to all participants equally."[20] All the various

15. Nicholas Smith, *Charles Taylor: Meaning, Morals and Modernity* (Hoboken, NJ: John Wiley & Sons, 2002), 98.

16. Taylor, *Sources of the Self*, 52.

17. "The background which makes sense of any given act is thus wide and deep. It doesn't include everything in our world, but the relevant sense-giving features can't be circumscribed; and because of this we can say that sense-giving draws on our whole world, that is, our sense of our whole predicament in time and space, among others and in history." Ibid, 174.

18. Taylor, *A Secular Age*, 159, 160.

19. Ibid.

differences and interpretations of the modern social imaginary include these four elements; however, all interpretations are not equal.

This commitment to fundamental equality and mutual benefit requires new ways of sociality; community is transformed but not eliminated. Among these new ways of sociality are a growing awareness of solidarity and a commitment to human rights. This new understanding of the individual and community is not only a precondition for universal human rights but also makes possible true solidarity among peoples. In addition, Taylor and Catholic social teaching reject the subtraction view of modernity in which human beings are by nature or essence individuals only. The subtraction view involves stripping away to get to the essence of what is truly human—individual freedom and rationality as the real human good glosses over the nuance and far-reaching developments of the modern period. Both neoclassical economics and many forms of utilitarianism adopt a vision of liberty that says, "A man is free when there are no obstacles in his path," and they see self-love as the motivation for human action.[21] "The logic of the subtraction story is something like this: once we slough off our concern with serving God, or attending to any other transcendent reality, what we're left with is human good, and that is what modern societies are concerned with."[22] This theory of modernity is fundamentally incorrect for two reasons. First, its basic assumption that human beings are essentially individuals and not social is mistaken, and, second, it glosses over the incredible change represented by the modern order.

While modern society has gone through *the great disembedding* from premodern hierarchical structures and identities, the individual remains deeply embedded in the new modern order of mutual obligation in which freedom and self-determination become central to morality: "To be really self-determining I must recover contact with my own authentic self, with the voice within, which is also the voice of conscience."[23] From this, Kant moves rationality to the center, arguing that "acting morally is acting with a certain goal, that of conforming my will to reason. But this is not a goal like any other, which could be identified with a certain class of external outcomes of action. Rather we have to think of it as a formal goal."[24] Thus, for Kant, "to have moral worth an action must be done from duty," not desire.[25] Rationality becomes the one thing that

20. Ibid, 171.

21. Charles Taylor, "Kant's Theory of Freedom," in *Philosophical Papers*, vol. 2: *Philosophy and the Human Sciences*, 319.

22. Taylor, *A Secular Age*, 572.

23. Taylor, "Kant's Theory of Freedom," 321.

24. Ibid, 322.

imposes obligations on us and has dignity; only rational agents have dignity. Furthermore, since we are rational agents among other rational agents, "rational demands are universal and thus require universal recognition."[26] Taken literally and narrowly, this understanding of both freedom and rationality distorts the vision of the human person and community so that human rights and solidarity compete with each other.[27]

Nominal assent to the claim that rational agency is to be respected above all else without a practical commitment to the social matrix necessary for its substantive use is hollow and inconsistent. Taylor rejects the narrow and individualistic interpretations of modernity and instead reinterprets and refocuses key insights to include the complicated social matrix that gave rise to and sustains modernity. He explains, "I am arguing that the free individual of the West is only what he is by virtue of the whole society and civilization which brought him to be and which nourishes him."[28] Furthermore, "to be an individual is not to be a Robinson Crusoe, but to be placed in a certain way among other humans"; this social matrix remains distinctively modern because "what we may learn is to be an individual, to have our own opinions, and attain our own relation to God, our own conversion experience."[29] Taylor, along with Catholic social teaching, offers a more holistic interpretation of the modern social imaginary than Enlightenment liberalism alone. Thus, as this book argues, human rights and solidarity are not rivals but intimately linked in the human person.

To develop a fuller philosophical anthropology, Taylor rejects the standard rhetoric of individualism by redefining key terms and examining the sundry ways in which the modern self is deeply embedded in a distinctive modern liberal world of human rights, mutual benefit, and equality.[30] Arguing for a

25. Immanuel Kant, *Grounding for the Metaphysics of Morals* 3rd edition (Cambridge, MA: Hackett, 1993), 16

26. Taylor, "Kant's Theory of Freedom," 328.

27. The distinction between Kant and Catholic social thought will be important for dialogue with Amartya Sen and the practical implementation of human rights as well as pinpointing concretely where Catholic social thought adds to human rights and development discourse.

28. Charles Taylor, "Atomism," in *Philosophical Papers*, vol. 2: *Philosophy and the Human Sciences*, 206.

29. Taylor, *Modern Social Imaginaries*, 65.

30. Taylor redefines the term *individualism* as "a moral idea, doesn't mean ceasing to belong at all—that's the individualism of anomie and breakdown—but imagining oneself as belonging to an even wider and more impersonal entities: the state, the movement, the community of human kind." Ibid., 160. It is clear that this flows from his assertion that dignity and respect for others comes with an obligation to belong. Instead of involving the breakdown of communities, modern individualism involves the extending of boundaries of community, something that becomes crucial not only for the project of

situated freedom that includes positive freedom, Taylor explains, "We cannot say that someone is free, on a self-realization view, if he is totally unrealized, if for instance, he is totally unaware of his potential, if fulfilling it has never even arisen as a question for him, or if he is paralyzed by the fear of breaking some norm."[31] As the previous sentence indicates, there can often be internal barriers to exercising freedom (such as fear); thus, one problem with a purely negative conception of freedom is that it focuses solely on external barriers. The modern individual needs to learn how to be an individual agent. Without being socially embedded in a modern community, the human being has no framework from which to act. Any truly human concept of self-sufficiency must account for our radically social existence. Moreover, any coherent and substantive theory of human rights must reflect this deep social embeddedness. This element in Taylor's work is particularly important for Catholic social teaching. A key example of this is the right to development. According to Catholic social teaching, "the right to development must be seen as a dynamic interpenetration of all those fundamental human rights upon which the aspirations of individuals and nations are based" (JM 1.2).

This civilization of human rights, equality, and mutual regard not only provides the social context for the modern individual to develop and flourish, but also imposes particular responsibilities on us. If these capacities are worthy of respect, then there is a responsibility to develop them, and, once they are recognized in another, there is a responsibility to create the conditions for their development by others.[32] An obligation to foster human capacities of freedom and agency already necessarily moves beyond the realm of purely negative duties, as emphasized in *Pacem in Terris*.

Once again, the right to development in *Populorum Progressio* is a key example. The ethical demand is simple: if freedom and agency are worthy of respect, then "I ought to become the kind of agent who is capable of authentic conviction, that I ought to be true to my own convictions and not live a lie or self-delusion . . . that I ought to in certain circumstances to help foster this capacity in others, that I ought to bring up my children to have it, that I ought not to inhibit it in others by influencing them towards a facile and shallow complaisance."[33] This is common and integral to our understanding of

universal human rights but also of solidarity. In particular, it can provide a mechanism for a global common good or global solidarity, as well as a philosophical grounding for the integrated approach to human rights and community found within Catholic social teaching in the previous chapter.

31. Taylor, "Atomism," 213.
32. Ibid, 194.
33. Ibid.

parenthood. Education and human development indicate that children need to be taught how to develop reason, freedom, and self-determining agency. We need others in order to develop as full human beings. Most generally, this is an acknowledgment that people need family.[34]

Families are central but not sufficient. The kind of freedom in which I am capable of conceiving alternatives and of self-realization, where I decide what I really want, what I must do, and so forth cannot arise purely from the family; it requires an entire civilization.[35] In order to teach this type of agency and self-determining freedom, the family must first have existed in a particular type of civilization. Furthermore, this process is not limited to children, although they provide a clear and easy example of our social dependence. We do not become isolated individuals in adulthood, and our obligation to belong does not end once we have developed self-determining freedom. Our obligation extends not only to our children but to future generations: "Future generations will need this civilization to reach these aspirations; and if we affirm their worth, we have an obligation to make them available to others. This obligation is only increased if we ourselves have benefitted from this civilization and have been enabled to become free agents ourselves."[36]

Notice the similarity in this obligation to the injunction of *Populorum Progressio* in the previous chapter. According to Pope Paul VI, "it is not just certain individuals who are called to this fullness of development. . . . We have inherited from past generations and we have benefited from the work of our contemporaries: for this reason, we have obligations toward all. . . . The reality of human solidarity which as a benefit for us also imposes a duty" (PP 17). The understanding of duty and obligation emphasized in Taylor's philosophical anthropology helps fill out their emphasis in Catholic social teaching. The duties of human rights then flow into our understanding of solidarity. This idea of mutual dependence between individuals and the community including an obligation to future generations is central to the relationship of human rights and solidarity. What then is the civilization required for developing persons in social solidarity and with substantial exercise of human rights?

THE OBLIGATION TO BELONG AND IMPLICATIONS FOR HUMAN RIGHTS

"Persons always live in relationships. We come from others, we belong to others, and our lives are enlarged by our encounter with others."

34. Ibid, 203.
35. Ibid. 204.
36. Ibid, 206.

Pope Francis, Lumen Fidei 38

In the modern moral order, "our whole view of ourselves, based upon our modern understanding of morality, and an ordered, disciplined society of mutual benefit, is that we have moved (in some favored countries) and are moving (in other less favored ones) to a civilization which entrenches democracy and human rights."[37] The order of mutual benefit is meant to secure freedom for individuals in the form of rights. Furthermore, these rights are to be equal and universal. Taylor is clear: "Discovering my own identity doesn't mean that I work it out in isolation, but that I negotiate it through dialogue, partly overt, partly internal, with others" (as evidenced by the earlier examples of language and education).[38] A commitment to universal human rights, then, must be understood relationally. Thus, a descriptive starting point for solidarity is the dialogical nature of the self, which is also a condition of being a self at all.

The good of the community, as a whole, is essential because it is a necessary condition for the development of individual human agents. If we do not begin with an adequate and accurate philosophical anthropology, we cannot achieve a substantive and realistic theory of human rights. A commitment to universal human rights must be a commitment to human persons, which means a commitment to communities. Taylor argues that, along with a commitment to the equal dignity of individuals, there must be a commitment to a *politics of recognition* in which the distinctiveness of communities and groups is protected. What then does this mean for the relationship between human rights and solidarity? If we benefited from this modern moral order of human rights, then, according to Taylor, we have a responsibility to and for this culture or civilization. But how far does this responsibility extend? Does this responsibility help us further understand the demands of solidarity? Taylor understands the modern self as involving a commitment to universal human rights, which in turn requires a commitment to global solidarity and thus provides a helpful philosophical explanation for Catholic social teaching's approach. It is crucial to the future of human rights and to Catholic social thought that this includes a rigorous philosophy of situated or socially embedded freedom. By examining the human person within communities, including the one human community as a whole, we begin to see that our responsibility for others extends beyond our interpersonal encounters to the distant neighbor. The obligation to sustain, protect, and promote the social matrix required for the substantive exercise

37. Taylor, *A Secular Age*, 691.
38. Taylor, *Politics of Recognition*, 34.

of human rights must be global (we will take up the specific question of responsibility in the next chapter).

One of the empirical observations of the last fifty years (as noted by Paul VI, John Paul II, and Benedict XVI) is the growing awareness of interdependence and human dignity. At the end of *A Secular Age*, Taylor acknowledges that "our age makes higher demands of solidarity and benevolence on people today than ever before. Never before have people been asked to stretch out so far, and so consistently, so systematically, so as a matter of course, to the stranger outside the gates."[39] As this becomes universal, the implicit obligations to uphold and foster this modern social imaginary must extend to the stranger. What is perhaps most radical in both Catholic social teaching and Taylor's understanding of the modern social imaginary is the insistence that if I have benefited from this modern order of human rights, then I have an obligation to foster, sustain, and promote that for others—even strangers across the globe. This, first and foremost, is a challenge to those who have substantive exercise of human rights. At the same time, however, motivation within the order of mutual benefit is both fragile and debated. If freedom and human rights are understood individualistically, then providing strong motivation for solidarity is a problem. Human rights and universal justice "have become part of our self-image, our sense of our own worth. And alongside this, we feel a sense of satisfaction and superiority when we contemplate others," which is dangerous because "a solidarity ultimately driven by the giver's own sense of moral superiority is a whimsical and fickle thing. We are far in fact from the universality and unconditionality which our moral outlook prescribes."[40] Moving toward this universality requires recognition of people as agents of collective empowerment and the role of common action.[41] The community and common life have value beyond simply creating the physical or intellectual conditions for individuals. Once again, solidarity as well as human rights are located in the dialogical nature of the human person.

Recognizing the diversity of community to which we belong is crucial to this approach. Diversity and uniqueness are not simply a matter of individuals or cultures. Communities have distinctive and valuable identities on every level, and it is possible to have a commitment to equal respect and universal human rights that continues to respect difference without sacrificing commitment to human dignity. Detailing the complexities of Taylor's communal understanding of human agency, self, narrative identity, and the modern social

39. Taylor, *A Secular Age*, 695.
40. Taylor, *A Secular Age*, 696.
41. Ibid, 579.

imaginary demonstrates the elements of a philosophical anthropology that grounds the necessary and intrinsic connection between human rights and solidarity. Thus, because of who we are, "there can be no progress toward the complete development of man without the simultaneous development of all humanity in the spirit of solidarity" (PP 43).

Claims of the universality of human rights without an obligation to belong to the human community remain abstract and cannot be sustained over the course of generations. Solidarity is a condition of possibility for the realization of a moral order of mutual benefit—on the level of individual human rights and on the level of the rights of communities. This is why Catholic social thought always pairs rights with responsibilities (or duties) and why Taylor stresses the social embeddedness of the modern individual. The narrative identity of both the authentically human person and an authentically human community requires human rights and solidarity. You cannot fully realize one without the other, in large part because of what it means to be human.

Modernity as examined here focuses on human goods: "It is true that a great deal of our political and moral life is focused on human ends: human welfare, human rights, human flourishing, equality between human beings. Indeed our public life, in societies which are secular in a familiar modern sense, is exclusively concerned with human goods. And our age is certainly unique in human history in this respect."[42] Taylor's contention is that this focus on human good does not have to be antithetical to a theological perspective—solidarity is a key example of this. In highlighting the fragility of our secular philosophical motivations behind solidarity, Taylor acknowledges that there are foundations for a commitment to solidarity outside of exclusive humanism. Christianity has a theological foundation for solidarity and diversity in the belief that human persons are created *imago dei*; "being made in the image of God, as a feature of each human being, is not something that can be characterized just by reference to this being alone. Our being in the image of God is also our standing among others in the stream of love, which is that facet of God's life we try to grasp, very inadequately in speaking of the Trinity."[43] While Taylor provides a robust philosophy of the person linking human rights and solidarity, the theology of the Trinity and *imago dei* operative in Catholic social teaching illuminates why this view of the person is essential for who we are as children of God created in God's own image.

42. Ibid., 569.

43. Ibid., 702. Cf. Charles Taylor, *A Catholic Modernity?: Charles Taylor's Marianist Award Lecture, with responses by William M. Shea, Rosemary Luling Haughton, George Marsden, and Jean Bethke Elshtain* (Oxford: Oxford University Press, 1999).

Human Persons and Community as *Imago Dei* and *Imago Trinitatis*

Catholic social thought, as well as Christian theology more broadly, begins all discussions of human dignity and human rights with the theological claim that all human persons are created in the image and likeness of God. Latent and often unexamined within the theology of the *imago dei*, however, is the theological claim that the one God is triune. How does belief in the Trinity change our understanding of human persons as *imago dei*? What does it mean to say that human persons and human communities are *imago trinitatis*? Using the biblical theology of the *imago dei*, insights of feminist Trinitarian theologians, and the theology of covenant, I seek to develop a theological anthropology that grounds both human rights and solidarity in our creation in the image and likeness of God.

Imago Dei, Trinity, and Covenant

> *"Then God said, 'Let us make humankind in our image, according to our likeness; . . . So God created humankind, in his image, in the image of God he created them; male and female he created them."*
> Gen. 1:26-27

> *"God did not create man for life in isolation, but for the formation of social unity, so also 'it has pleased God to make men holy and save them not merely as individuals, without bond or link between them, but by making them into a single people . . .'"*
> Gaudium et Spes, 32

The unconditional love necessary to sustain and motivate solidarity is "not conditional on the worth realized in you just as an individual or even realizable in you alone," but is based every human person's being made in the image and likeness of God.[44] Human relationality and personhood, then, is not only a matter of being related to one another within a social matrix but also being related to the triune God, in whose image and likeness we were created.[45] As Catholic feminist theologian Elizabeth A. Johnson, CSJ, highlights, "In the

---

44. Taylor, *A Catholic Modernity?*, 35.

45. Doctrinally, Christian belief and talk about God as Trinity, however incomplete and limited, must be predicated upon equality, mutuality, and reciprocity in order to maintain in balance both God as one and God as the Trinitarian communion of three persons.

end, the Trinity provides a symbolic picture of totally shared life at the heart of the universe. It subverts duality into multiplicity. Mutual relationship of different equals appears as the ultimate paradigm of personal and social life."[46] The Trinity provides insights not only for understanding the human person but from which to engage in social critique of communities of persons. If the Trinity provides the ultimate paradigm of personal and social life, then it is integral for both human rights and solidarity. Beyond the connection between the Trinity and our understanding of personhood, the theology of covenant illuminates the necessary connection between human rights and solidarity by providing a bridge between statements about the Trinity and those about the human community.

Clarifying and deepening the theological anthropology behind Catholic social teaching's commitment to human rights and solidarity requires drawing on several additional themes found in Scripture. I contend that there are two key passages, Gen. 1:26–7 and John 17:20-22, that are crucial to a theological understanding of human dignity and to the larger project of integrating human rights and solidarity. In order to be grounded in the human person, both human rights and solidarity must be understood as flowing directly from our creation in the image and likeness of God. According to Genesis: "Then God said, 'Let us make humankind in our image, according to our likeness. . . . So God created humankind, in his image, in the image of God he created them; male and female he created them" (Gen. 1:26–27).[47] The foundation of human dignity, Genesis provides a strong commitment not only to the creation of all human persons in the *imago dei* but also the insistence that we are social beings from creation. The obvious justification for that sociality is the creation of male and female in the story—from the very beginning there is community. *Gaudium et Spes* explains, "Their companionship produces the primary form of interpersonal communion. For his innermost nature man is a social being, and unless he relates himself to others, he can neither live nor develop his potential" (GS 12). Approaching the *imago dei* in this way emphatically establishes that all human persons, male and female, are equally created in the image and likeness of God. Furthermore, there is a deep recognition that the human person alone and solitary is incomplete. We are not simply individuals who *should* choose to enter into community and relationship. While the freedom of the individual person allows for a number of

---

46. Elizabeth Johnson, *She Who Is* (New York: Crossroads, 1998), 222.

47. Cf. *Sirach* 17:1-3, 10-12, 14, which also attends to humanity's creation in the image of God, the establishing of the covenant, and the law concerning one's neighbor. In particular, placing the three within the same treatment of the relationship between God and humanity illustrates the continuity between the sections of this chapter.

choices concerning how, to whom, and when we are in active relationship with those around us, to be a human person created in the image of God is to be in community and relationship, and this is not something from which we are able to opt out.

From the perspective of Christian theology, then, the model of this dynamic relationship involves both theological anthropology and Trinitarian theology. The question becomes how it is that we are created in the image and likeness of the Trinity. This connection between the relationality of divine persons and humanity as *imago dei* is further emphasized in Jesus' prayer "that they might be one . . . as we are one" (John 17:21-22). Moreover, according to International Theological Commission, "In the Christian perspective, this personal identity that is at once an orientation to the other is founded essentially on the Trinity of divine persons. God is not a solitary person but a communion of three persons. [yet still, one divine nature.]. . . In effect, no person is as such alone in the universe, but is always constituted with others and is summoned to form a community with them."[48] Thus, human persons are in the image and likeness of God "by reason of their capacity for community with other persons."[49] Furthermore, inherent within this concept of personhood is the notion that "as human beings we are capable of participating in the very humanity of other people, and because of this every human being can be our *neighbor.*"[50]

Within Catholic social teaching, interpreting the communal aspect of the *imago dei* from Scripture tends to focus on marriage and the family.[51] Ideally, the

---

48. International Theological Commission "Communion and Stewardship: Human Persons Created in the Image of God" (2004), #41, http://www.vatican.va/roman_curia/congregations/cfaith/cti_documents/rc_con_cfaith_doc_20040723_communion-stewardship_en.html.

49. Karol Wojtyla, "The Family as a Community of Persons," in *Person and Community: Selected Essays,* trans. Theresa Sandok, OSM (New York: Peter Lang, 1993), 318.

50. Karol Wojtyla, "Participation or Alienation?" in *Person and Community,*200.

51. This is also evidenced throughout the International Theological Commission's document on the *imago dei*: "Communion and Stewardship: Human Persons Created in the Image of God," 2004. Moreover, another example of this is the *Compendium of the Social Doctrine of the Church,* which states, "The pages of the first book of Sacred Scripture, which describe the creation of man and woman in the image and likeness of God (cf. *Gen* 1:26-27), contain a fundamental teaching with regard to the identity and the vocation of the human person. They tell us that the creation of man and woman is a free and gratuitous act of God; that man and woman, because they are free and intelligent, represent the 'thou' created by God and that only in relationship with him can they discover and fulfill the authentic and complete meaning of their personal and social lives; that in their complementarities and reciprocity they are the image of Trinitarian Love in the created universe; that to them, as the culmination of creation, the Creator has entrusted the task of ordering created nature according to his design (cf. Gen 1:28)."

family functions descriptively to illustrate this community, which is more than a sum of the individuals and which is not based on mutual self-interest. This is because the fundamental insight is love and self-gift. Then, in the language of human rights and Catholic social thought, "to maintain that the human being is created in the image of God is to proclaim that the human being is capable of self-gift. The human person is the point at which creation is able to respond by giving oneself in return. The fundamental human right is the right to give oneself away to another and ultimately to the Other" (God).[52] While this is most often examined in Christian ethics as beginning with the distinction between male/female and with marriage, I contend that the family more broadly provides the best analogical starting point for understanding the relationality inherent within human persons as in the image of the Trinity, as demonstrating self-gift not self-interest, and as integrating both the Genesis creation account and Jesus' prayer in the Gospel of John.[53] The family, broadly and comprehensively understood, is intergenerational and ever expanding. The family as community integrates relationships and obligations in the past, present, future generations.

Human persons grow, develop, and foster relationships throughout their life. Community then is a constitutive part of what it means to be human. As such, human persons becomes more or less free, more or less authentically human in their relationships to God and others. Our humanity, as in the image of God, is not only a matter of creation but also places a claim on us. Deep within Catholic ethics is the call to become more fully human, to more

Catholic Church, Pontificium Consilium de Iustitia et Pace, *Compendium of the Social Doctrine of the Church* (Vatican City: Veritas, 2005), #36. Within this reflection is the dual focus of "freedom and intelligence" as well as the recognition that reciprocity is central to our being in the image of Trinitarian love. The family is the obvious starting point for Catholic social teaching on community for many reasons. Deeply ingrained within Catholic theology is a view of the family as the first community, the domestic church, and the bedrock of larger society. According to John Paul II, "of all systems of relationships, the family is the one in which we can perhaps most easily and fully perceive not only the common but also the specifically communal character of human existence." Wojtyla, "Family as a Community of Persons," 323.

52. Michael J. Himes and Kenneth R. Himes, "The Trinity and Human Rights," in *Fullness of Faith: The Public Significance of Theology* (New York, Paulist, 1993), 59.

53. In his exposition of Genesis, biblical scholar Sibley Towner concludes, "In summary, then, if we see the image of the divine in the maleness and femaleness of humankind, it is not in their sexual junction *per se*. That comes as a separate divine authorization of what would in any case be necessary for survival, multiplication and dominion. 'Image' is manifested in their very plurality and consequent fellowship." W. Sibley Towner, "Clones of God: *Genesis* 1:26-28 and the Image of God in the Hebrew Bible," *Interpretation* 59, no. 4 (2005): 349.

fully and faithfully image God in the world, to create more human conditions for persons and communities. An explicit demand of the *imago dei*, then, is the acknowledgment of our common humanity, which has deep implications in both human rights and solidarity. What this practically requires, however, is a more difficult question. Moreover, while the family provides a starting framework, the family itself must be examined critically and evaluated in light of the Trinity as model. The Trinity as a community of persons can and should provide a clear and challenging paradigm from which to evaluate Christian communities, including the family.

Recent waves in feminist theology and theological anthropology have returned to the Trinity to recover a more relational understanding of both God and the human person and thus to deepen our understanding of human persons in the *image and likeness of God*.[54] As Elizabeth Johnson points out, "God is not a person in the modern sense. God transcends what we understand to be person as the source of all that is personal and thus is not less than personal."[55] As such, the equality, mutuality, and reciprocity of the persons of the Trinity are revelatory for the participation and community to which humanity is called. Out of the experience of "God's gracious ways active in the world through Jesus Christ and the Spirit," where we discover "the fundamental revelation about God's own being as a self-giving communion of love," the language of person developed

54. Catherine LaCugna, *God for Us: The Trinity and Christian Life* (San Francisco: Harper Collins, 1991). Traditionally, following Augustine, Catholic theology understood the connection between the Trinity and the image of God as a matter of seeing ways the Trinity is imprinted on the human soul. As Catherine LaCugna explains, "Augustine's premise is that the soul is created in the image and after the likeness of God (Gen 1:26). The journey of the soul is cyclic: the soul loves God and seeks to return to God. Moreover, in drawing the soul back to Godself, God bestows on the soul true knowledge of itself. Thus, if God is a Trinity, then the soul must resemble that which it images and that to which it seeks to return." (93). From this Augustinian approach, which "charted human consciousness as the method for understanding the Trinity" (82), Western Trinitarian thought placed a strong emphasis on the individual and rationality. The major problem in Augustine's quest is the purely individual focus, which when approached via the Enlightenment distorts the connection between person as applied to God and to humans (103). As a result, the self has come to be understood as an isolated center of consciousness, and as LaCugna highlights, "This fits well with the idea that God is personal, but not at all with the idea that God is three persons. Three persons defined in this way would amount to three gods, three beings who act independently, three conscious individuals" (250).

55. Johnson, *She Who Is*, 203. In her work, Johnson relies heavily on the theology of Karl Rahner, SJ, who stated: "Person does not mean 'essence' or 'nature' but the actual unique reality of a spiritual being, an undivided whole existing independently and not interchangeable with any other. This reality is the reality of a being, which belongs to itself and is therefore its own end in itself. It is the concrete form taken by the freedom of a spiritual being, one, which is, based in its inviolable dignity." Karl Rahner, "Person," in *Encyclopedia of Theology* (New York: Seabury Press, 1975), 1207.

as the best among inadequate languages that cannot but fail to capture the experience of God. For the first believers, "we might say that they experienced the saving God in a threefold way as beyond them, with them, and within them, that is as transcendent, as present historically in the person of Jesus, and as present in the Spirit within their community. These were all encounters with only one God."[56] While all *god-talk* or language about the Trinity is analogical, there are key theological insights from this encounter with the triune God that illuminate the human person as *imago dei* and as a bearer of human rights called to solidarity.[57]

Relationality, equality, and mutuality emerge—out of the commitment to the Father, Son, and Holy Spirit as three equally divine persons in the one triune God—as three essential characteristics of Trinitarian monotheism. Each person is radically equal to each other, and "the nature of the divine relations is such that the persons do not lose their distinctiveness by being so related. On the contrary, the relations not only bond the persons but establish them in personal uniqueness."[58] Referencing Augustine, Johnson emphasizes that there is no subordination in the Trinity. This is the beauty of the metaphor of *perichoresis*, which, "when applied to the life of the Trinity this metaphor indicates that each of the 'persons' dynamically moves around the others, interweaves with others in a circling of divine life. While remaining distinct, the three cohere in each other in a communion of love."[59] This unity is at the foundation of the human person's ability to truly be in community, to be *neighbor*, and to participate in the humanity of another. It is thus a basic requirement not only of human rights but also of solidarity.

For God, to be is to be in relation, but there is a danger, as Johnson and others note, in any language we use to talk about God and intra-Trinitarian life. All language is analogy; all language is ultimately inadequate. One danger that emerges, in the wake of post-Enlightenment understandings of the person, is that using the language of *person* applied to the Trinity makes the Trinity appear tritheistic. It is important, however, to retrieve the rich theological foundation for *person* despite its limitations and post-Enlightenment connotations. Just as we cannot relinquish "the self" to modern individualism, so too theological ethics cannot afford to lose the connection between human personhood and

56. Ibid., 204.

57. For more on analogy and "God-talk" see Brian Davies, *The Thought of Thomas Aquinas* (Oxford: Clarendon, 1993), ch. 4; and Johnson, *Quest for the Living God*.

58. Johnson, *She Who Is*, 219.

59. Johnson, *Quest for the Living God*, 214. This *perichoresis* is used as the image of Trinity contra the emphasis of the monarchy of the father.

divine personhood. Our ethics, as Benedict XVI notes, "is illuminated in a striking way by the relationship between the persons in the Trinity within the one Divine Substance" (CV 54). In order to maintain the connection between our Trinitarian theology and our theological anthropology, in particular the implications of human beings as *imago dei*, it is necessary to adapt and reclaim *person*.

How then does one define personhood in such a way as to maintain some real analogical connection between human personhood and divine personhood? Catherine LaCugna offers a multifaceted definition of personhood as the foundation for an understanding of persons in communion. Each of these points applies to both divine and human personhood, insofar as either is an instance of personhood. For the purpose of a theological anthropology that deepens our understanding of *imago dei*, human rights, and solidarity, there are five constitutive elements of personhood predicated upon a communion of equality, mutuality, and reciprocity. First, "Persons are essentially interpersonal, intersubjective."[60] The focus on relationality and intersubjectivity is important to the person's ability to offer a genuine gift of self in relationships and be open to such a gift from another. The next two related constants, "a person is an ineffable, concrete, unique, and unrepeatable" nature and "the person is the foundation of a nature" directly move from our understanding of God to that of human relationships.[61] An all-encompassing wholeness to the full understanding of personhood comes out clearly in both LaCugna and Johnson. Johnson explains that "relationality is the principle that at once constitutes each Trinitarian person as unique and distinguishes one from another."[62]

In a manner similar to Taylor's philosophical approach to freedom as including positive freedom, freedom for a person from a theological perspective "consists in being free-for, free-toward others, poised in the balance between self-possession and other-orientation."[63] Authentic human freedom is theologically located in the balance between *self-possession* and *self-gift*. In part, this is why feminist ethics "rejects the ideal of non-relational autonomy as deficiently human."[64] Finally, from this understanding of freedom and the conviction that the Trinity is a very practical Christian doctrine, the fifth constitutive element asserts that "living as persons in communion, in right

---

60. LaCugna, *God for Us*, 288–89.

61. Ibid., 289–90.

62. Johnson, *She Who Is*, 216.

63. LaCugna, *God for Us*, 290.

64. Johnson, *She Who Is*, 68.

relationship, is the meaning of salvation and the ideal of Christian faith."[65] The Trinity, then, is a practical doctrine for both human rights and solidarity. Thus, "that they may be one as we are" one stands as an eschatological vision pointing the human community toward solidarity.

This is confirmed by God's own interaction with humanity through the covenants, which provide a vertical bridge between the intra-Trinitarian life and the communion of persons among themselves and with God.[66] A covenant is a solemn agreement in which something is offered and accepted in love; "every promise of this kind binds the person who promises, and offers him or her the trust and faithfulness, or partners to the bond."[67] For Christianity, the biblical covenants establish not only our relationship to God— the possibility of friendship with God—but also God's love and commitment to creation by entering into relationships with humanity, communities, and successive generations. God chooses to enter into relationship with the community or people as evidenced by four major Biblical covenants (Noah, Abraham, Moses, and Jesus).[68] Through attention to these covenants and God's claim on us, covenant establishes the obligation to belong, recognizing communal identity while preserving individual identity and responsibility. One can see this building to Matthew's account of the last judgment, where we are told that we will individually be judged based upon our life in community. Respect for human rights and living authentic solidarity, then, emerges as a concrete way to judge whether or not we are living out *imago dei* and participating in the humanity of our neighbor.

The flood narrative in Genesis 6–9 culminates with God entering into a covenant with Noah, in which God promises, "I will never again curse the ground because of humankind" (8:21), offers the rainbow as the sign "of the covenant that I have established between me and all flesh that is on this

---

65. LaCugna, *God for Us*, 292.

66. The International Theological Commission links the *imago dei,* Trinitarian communion, and covenant stating, "The triune God has revealed his plan to share the communion of Trinitarian life with persons created in his image. Indeed, it is for the sake of this Trinitarian communion that human persons are created in the divine image. It is precisely this radical likeness to the triune God that is the basis for the possibility of the communion of creaturely beings with the uncreated persons of the Blessed trinity." "Communion and Stewardship," #25.

67. Jürgen Moltmann, *Experiences in Theology: Ways and Forms of Christian Theology*, (Minneapolis, MN: Fortress Press, 2000), 95.

68. This is not an exhaustive list, as the Davidic covenant could be included in a treatment of covenantal theology. However, I am limiting my treatment to the biblical covenants Moltmann specifically addresses in his use of covenantal theology to support and condition a Christian understanding of human rights.

earth" (9:17), and alludes to the importance of human life, "for in his own image God made humankind" (9:6). Biblical scholar Sibley Towner explains, "Actually, Gen 1:26-7 and its echoes in 5:1-2 and 9:6 point human relationships in three directions. Of course, human beings are related to their creator, God. . . . Second, we related to each other, beginning with simple fellowship of male and female. This we express in love and loyalty."[69] And, third, we are placed in relationship to the rest of creation. Thus this covenant is understood to incorporate all of humanity and to demonstrate that all are capable of responding to God. The second covenant, with Abraham and Sarah (Gen. 17:4-9), and the third, through Moses (Exod. 19:5-6), establishes a special relationship between God and a particular people.[70] Both make demands and promises, and both emphasize God's relationship with the community through an ever-expanding and lasting covenant. Rescuing the Israelites from slavery in Egypt and establishing the law, God reveals Godself in the Mosaic covenant as loving and liberating his people. *Gaudium et Spes* uses this covenant to illustrate God's liberating action, which is simultaneously personal and communal.

Because of the gift of creation *imago dei* and in response to personal relationships to both others and to God, the human person owes it to God to live a life of equality, mutuality, and reciprocity in recognition of the equal dignity of all human persons. In practice, this duty involves human rights. Thus, German Protestant theologian Jürgen Moltmann argues, "In the designation of the human being to be the image of God, the right of God to all human beings is expressed. The human rights to life, freedom, community and self-determination mirror God's right to the human being because the human being is destined to be God's image in all conditions and relationship of life."[71] God enters into relationship with people, and central to human dignity is the ability of the human person to respond to God. The International Theological Commission states, "Created in the image of God to share in the communion of Trinitarian life, human beings . . . are so constituted as to be able freely to embrace this communion."[72]

Solidarity as an integral facet of both the *imago dei* and covenant with God is emphasized by the fulfillment of the covenant in the New Testament.

69. Towner, "Clones of God," 349.

70. "You shall be the ancestor of a multitude of nations. . . . I will establish my covenant between me and you, and your offspring after you throughout their generations, for an everlasting covenant" (Gen. 17:4-9).

71. Jürgen Moltmann, "Ecumenical Dialogue on Human Rights," in *On Human Dignity: Political Theology and Ethics* (Minneapolis, MN: Fortress Press, 1984) 17.

72. International Theological Commission, #44.

Throughout his ministry, Jesus challenges us to "love the Lord your God with all your heart, and with all your soul, and with all your strength, and with all your mind; and your neighbor as yourself . . . do this and you will live" (Luke 10:27-28). Love of neighbor is clearly a condition of living in right relationship with God. This call to solidarity, however, is not limited to our family, friends, local community, or nation. Who is my neighbor? According to the Gospels, every human person is my neighbor (see, for instance, the parable of the Good Samaritan in Luke 10:30-37). This is further emphasized in the Gospel of Matthew's famous account of the last judgment:

> Come, you that are blessed by my Father, inherit the kingdom prepared for you from the foundation of the world; for I was hungry and you gave me food, for I was thirsty and you gave me something to drink, I was a stranger and you welcomed me, I was naked and you gave me clothing, I was sick and you took care of me, I was in prison and you visited me. Then the righteous will answer him, "Lord, when was it that we saw you hungry and gave you food, or thirsty and gave you something to drink?" . . . And the king will answer them, "Truly I tell you, just as you did it to one of the least of those who are members of my family, you did it to me." (Matt. 25:34-40)

There is much debate concerning the intention of Matthew's apocalyptic parable and the proper place of this passage within Christian ethics; however, the passage taken within the context of the Gospels as a whole challenges Christians to ask, who are the least among us today?[73] Faithful discipleship is conditioned by the answer to that question. While it is not in the language of rights or solidarity, the final judgment in Matthew 25 makes clear that within our modern moral order, fidelity to God is based on the acknowledgment of human rights and solidarity. We shall be judged on our living the Beatitudes, which, if we examine them within the context of human rights and solidarity, are among the most fundamental minimum conditions for participation in the community as persons in the image and likeness of God.

In examining the gospel, it is not my intention to reduce the Christian message or ministry to a matter of human rights. Living according to the gospel is a challenge that goes beyond the requirements of human rights. However, when authentic human rights and solidarity are understood as two sides of the

---

73. John R. Donahue, SJ, "The 'Parable' of the Sheep and the Goats: a Challenge to Christian Ethics," *Theological Studies* 47 (1986), p. 3-31.

same coin, the gospel account of the covenant, in Jesus, is a powerful reminder of both universal solidarity and the centrality of the economic and social rights. It is a reminder that all human persons are created in the image of God and are our neighbors; therefore, living in solidarity with the poor and marginalized is living in solidarity with Christ. And, as I argue throughout this book, living in solidarity is not possible without human rights. Through attention to the *imago dei* and Trinity, to be human created in the image of God is to be in a community of mutual, reciprocal love and equality. As such, the communion of persons in the Trinity is a model for how we ought to authentically live as a community of persons in the image of that Trinity. Thus, *imago dei* is also *imago trinitatis*.

In these covenants, fidelity to God is explicitly measured through the community's fidelity to both God and neighbor. Therefore, as Margaret Farley, RSM, concludes, "If the ultimate normative model for relationship between persons is the very life of the Trinitarian God, then a strong eschatological ethic suggests itself as a context for Christian justice . . . not only as a norm against which every pattern of relationship may be measured but as a goal to which every pattern of relationship is ordered."[74] In the dynamic of building community, for Christians, the Trinity itself serves as both the criterion of judgment and the goal of equality, mutuality, and reciprocity. This is a radical standard, and yet for Christian theology this normative calling is built into our very creation as *imago dei*. Just as Taylor's philosophical anthropology and the requisite social matrix do not allow a person to claim that some should reap the benefits of the modern human rights ethic but others should not, so too retrieving the idea of *imago dei* as *imago trinitatis* allows a focus on both the person and the community. To the universality of freedom and equality, Christian theological anthropology adds mutuality and reciprocity as integral to human dignity in relationships. What then are concrete implications for human rights and solidarity of this deepened and social understanding of the *imago dei* as *imago trinitatis*?

THEOLOGICAL IMPLICATIONS FOR HUMAN RIGHTS AND SOLIDARITY

"So that they may be one, as we are one, I in them and you in me, that they may become completely one, so that the world may know that you have sent me and have loved them even as you have loved me."
John 17:22–23

---

74. Margaret Farley, RSM, "New Patterns of Relationship," *Theological Studies* 36(4), 1975, p. 645–6.

How then ought I to live and develop as an image of God, who is Trinity and love? "God lives as a mystery of love. Human beings are created in the image of this God. Therefore, a life of integrity is impossible unless we also enter into the dynamic of love and communion with others."[75] If we begin from Scripture and the doctrine of the Trinity examined here, the question of how to live as the image of God is twofold. First, it is an individual one—as each and every human person is *imago dei* and has equal dignity. This aspect of human dignity or the *imago dei* is present in every defense and articulation of human rights. It is the "task" of Vatican II and Catholic social teaching: "the dignity of the human person finds its full confirmation in the very fact of revelation, for this fact signifies the establishing of contact between God and human beings, to the human being created in the image and likeness of God."[76] However, belief in the triune God adds another aspect of human personhood and creation as *imago dei*. When the Trinity is understood as a living relationship of divine persons in love, mutuality, reciprocity, and equality, we see not only that each individual is created in the image and likeness of God, but *we* are in the image and likeness of God. In *On Human Dignity*, Jürgen Moltmann emphasizes, "Only in human fellowship with other people is the human person truly an image of God."[77] Examining the *imago dei* from the perspective of sin, the International Theological Commission states that "sin affects the social dimension of the *imago dei*; it is possible to discern ideologies and structures which are objective manifestations of sin and which obstruct the realization of the image of God on the part of human beings."[78] I contend that this applies not only to individual persons but to the human community itself. Just as we speak of individual persons as being more fully human, leading a more fully human life and more fully imaging God, so it follows that we, as the human community, can more or less fully image God. This is the theological foundation for solidarity, a foundation that is not only compatible with human rights but mandates them.

Based on the firm belief that human persons are created in the image and likeness of the one triune God, I have sought to show in this chapter that it cannot be sufficient to understand the *imago dei* as purely individual. It cannot be sufficient to simply state that "I" am relational and therefore more or less fully image God in those relationships of my own choosing.

75. Johnson, *Quest for the Living God,* p. 222.

76. Wojtyla, 'On the Dignity of the Human Person," p. 179. Beyond the *imago dei*, the significance of this relationship culminates in the incarnation, the revelation that God became a human person.

77. Moltmann, *On Human Dignity: Political Theology and Ethics.* p. 25.

78. International Theological Commission, "Communion and Stewardship," #45.

Instead, the equality, mutuality, and reciprocity of human dignity clearly begin with the assertion that each and every human person is equal in dignity. The theological anthropology examined here clearly affirms the importance and dignity of each individual person, who is the bearer of rights and who is both responsive and responsible to God. At the same time, it denies the myth of the modern individual that understands the individual as isolated and possessing a freedom of choice that allows him or her to exist without relationships or only in relationships expressly chosen. While there are many situations, particularly those of personal abuse, in which affirmation of one's dignity mandates the breaking of a relationship with an individual or group, one does not then cease to be a relational being participating in many other communities, relationships, and so on. The individual human person as *imago dei* is only half the story. Given the communion and unity of the triune God, who created us in God's own image, we as community more or less fully image God in our various relationships. This begins with personal relationships, families, local communities, and churches but extends to our creation as one global human family.

In order to have a human rights ethic that reflects the dignity of the human person as created in the image and likeness of the Trinity, human rights cannot be understood individualistically. They cannot be simply *my* rights; if they are truly *human* rights, then each and every person must be a bearer of said rights. As such, the full realization of these rights, even for one individual, is related to the realization of these rights by the entire community of persons. Human rights, therefore, are not at odds with solidarity but require solidarity as a necessary component of their full realization. *Pacem in Terris* understands this in its assertion of the rights and responsibilities of individuals, communities, and nation-states. Recognizing the reality of interdependence and appreciating the need for subsidiarity, Pope John XXIII stresses each level of society as integral to the project of human rights. Theologically, this is because of the human dignity of each person as well as the dignity of the human community; both are integral to what it means to be created in the image and likeness of the triune God. Therefore, from the beginning, even without explicit theological argument and language, Catholic social teaching understood that any true realization of human rights must be mutual, equal, and reciprocal in our communal life, not just individually.

Developing an ethic of human rights and solidarity based on this theological anthropology demands that attention to how *we* image God underwrites our individual and communal actions, and not simply in words or in a nominal assertion of solidarity. To say that we, as children of God or as the one human family, more or less fully image God is to say that, as individuals, the extent to which we can image God is related to how faithfully or badly we live that image. How faithfully we, as community, provide witness to the image of God is a constant question for humans as created *imago dei*. Furthermore, my own ability to live in right relationship with God in covenant is dependent upon my living in right relationship with the human community, at its many levels.

PARTICIPATION IS THE KEY FOR HUMAN RIGHTS AND SOLIDARITY

The human person as an isolated, unsituated "self," truly detached from society, is an illusion. "To be an isolated, autonomous individual is, literally, to have no humanity, no identity, no self, to be no-thing, a no body," explains liberation theologian Roberto Goizueta. He continues, "For if personhood presupposes relationality, my humanity is defined by my relationships with others; I recognize myself as a self, as a person, only when I encounter or am encountered by another person."[79] Always embedded in a social matrix, the modern individual claims her agency, freedom, and universal and equal human rights. Far from being an isolated self, the modern person is dependent upon the modern social imaginary and, as such, has a profound obligation to belong: an obligation grounded in her debt to previous generations and responsibility to others both in present and future generations. As Goizueta explains, "Relationship is not something that 'happens to' someone, something one 'experiences,' in a passive way, or something one 'possesses'; it is something one *does*, the most basic form of human action since, through relationship we discover and live out our identity as intrinsically related beings."[80]

How does Taylor's philosophy of the person help illuminate the foundation and implications of Catholic social teaching's emphasis on the duty of solidarity? There is a basic mutuality assumed or required in the modern order of mutual benefit; however, many interpretations of this modern moral order, as demonstrated throughout this chapter, remain on the level of individuals. Given our dialogical identity, the obligation to belong has distinctive implications for what is required of us. Belonging involves more than recognition of another's humanity; it requires recognition that on some level we are in community together and are open to being changed and engaged by others. The value of freedom and rational agency as something universally worthy of respect,

79. Roberto Goizueta, "Community as the Birthplace of Self," in *Caminemos con Jesus: Toward a Hispanic/Latino Theology of Accompaniment* (Maryknoll, NY: Orbis, 2002), 50.

80. Goizueta, *Caminemos*, 72.

combined with the social dependence of rational agency, grounds an obligation to belong that extends beyond one's own family, local community, and culture. Our obligation to various levels of society is not identical; for example, we do not bear the same responsibility for developing the conditions of rational autonomous agency for persons across the world as we do for our own children. However, the obligation to belong is a clear way to understand the deep connection between rights and responsibilities, as well as the transference of interdependence to the moral plane, represented in Catholic social teaching. Belonging requires participation. And, as both Taylor and Goizueta understand the human person, there is an intimate connection between relationality and participation. The obligation to belong is one instance where the observable reality of relationality translates into the normative ethical claim of active participation.

The connection between relationality and participation is crucial to both the philosophical and theological anthropology behind Catholic social teaching. The return to the Trinity as a starting point for understanding personhood and humanity is largely focused around the language of relationality; however, not all theologians agree that *relationality* is the best way to characterize intra-Trinitarian life.[81] Despite this, David Cunningham and others point to a growing consensus about relationality within systematic Trinitarian theology.[82] Arguing against relationality in favor of *participation*, David S. Cunningham claims that relationality "lacks the sharp edge that might provide a serious and concrete analysis of the ethical implications of Trinitarian doctrine."[83] In arguing for participation over relationality, Cunningham overestimates the differences between the growing consensus, represented by LaCugna and Johnson, and his own position. Both Johnson and LaCugna are using relationality in an attempt to argue that there are serious ethical implications

81. LaCugna's Trinitarian theology and relational ontology is in contrast to the Trinitarian theologies of Karl Rahner and Karl Barth; in addition, her relational ontology has been challenged by theologians such as Nicholas Lash.

82. For an extensive treatment of this relational wave in systematic theology see Jennifer Anne Herrick, *Trinitarian Intelligibility—An Analysis of Contemporary Discussions: An Investigation of Western Academic Trinitarian Theology of the Late Twentieth Century* (Boca Raton, FL Universal, 2007).

83. David S. Cunningham, "Participation as a Trinitarian Virtue: Challenging the Relational Consensus," *Toronto Journal of Theology* 14, no. 1(1998), p. 10. He explains, "The contemporary emphasis on God's relationality has, at best, issued in an appeal for human beings to recognize the degree to which they are 'in relationship' to one another. By contrast, the focus on *participation* suggests that human beings are called to understand themselves not as 'individuals' who may (or may not) choose to enter into relationships, but rather as mutually indwelling and indwelt, and to such a degree that—echoing the mutual indwelling of the Three—all pretensions to wholly independent existence are abolished."

to Trinitarian doctrine. For Cunningham, "the idea of participation signifies
. . . that by which 'the Three are *mutually constitutive* of one another.'"[84] All
three scholars agree that, "in God, this 'complete mutual participation' means
that it is impossible to isolate any one of the Three without fundamentally
distorting the entire picture."[85] LaCugna, Johnson, and Cunningham all point
toward an integral, integrated relational person. The growing consensus about
relationality among Catholic feminist systematic theologians parallels a similar
emphasis on participation within Catholic social ethicists, as evidenced in the
work of Lisa Sowle Cahill, Margaret Farley, and David Hollenbach, SJ.[86]
Through the focus on equality, mutuality, and reciprocity as the standard by
which to evaluate relationality, relationality as it has been used here incorporates
the key aspects of the broader normative concept of participation as it is used
throughout the rest of this book.

Whether using the language of relationality or participation, the focus on
Trinitarian personhood is an effort to reclaim a theological anthropology that is
essential for human rights and solidarity. The Trinity enlightens not only our
understanding of the mystery of God but also who we are as human persons
in the image of that God. Elizabeth Johnson explains, "The mystery of God
is not an isolated monad but rather a living communion in relation with the
world. Nourished at the table of this love, the Church is drawn to the praxis of
justice so that all peoples and creatures may share in this communion."[87] In the
end, the doctrinal commitment that all human persons are created *imago dei* also
means that we are created *imago trinitatis.* This provides a clear starting point for
ethically evaluating any social order as well as for the challenge of the obligation
to belong; for "if the image of God is the ultimate reference point for the values
of a community, then the structure of the triune symbol stands as a profound
critique."[88]

Participation, as opposed to simply the fact of relationality, points to the
ethical claim that we can participate not only in the humanity of our neighbors

84. Herrick, *Trinitarian Intelligibility*, 142.

85. Cunningham, "Participation as a Trinitarian Virtue," 11–2.

86. Lisa Sowle Cahill, *Theological Bioethics: Participation, Justice, and Change* (Washington DC:
Georgetown University Press, 2005); Margaret Farley, *Compassionate Respect: A Feminist Approach to
Medical Ethics and Other Questions* (Milwaukee, WI: Paulist, 2002); and David Hollenbach, *The Global
Face of Public Faith: Politics, Human Rights, and Christian Ethics* (Washington, DC: Georgetown
University Press, 2003).

87. Elizabeth A. Johnson, CSJ, "Trinity: To Let the Symbol Sing Again," *Theology Today* 54, no. 3
(1997): 299.

88. Johsnon, *She Who Is*, 223.

but in their oppression, scapegoating, and dehumanization. In sacrificing any group of human persons we are sacrificing our own ability, individually and collectively, to more fully and faithfully image God, and, therefore, we stunt our ability to develop and live more fully human lives. This is not and cannot be limited to the ways in which we actively or passively sanction or overlook oppression. It is not a matter of establishing universal guilt but about establishing a universal bond—that we are one human family. This universal bond, this challenge of participation, abolishes previous limits of who counts within the obligation to belong, creating instead levels of community beginning with the family but extending to the universal, the one human family. Based on this theological anthropology, the marginalization, exploitation, and other human rights violations of individuals or communities of human persons are violations of human dignity and, as such, are an affront to the dignity of every human person. Solidarity is not simply a matter of interdependence but recognition that we are created in the image and likeness of God. As a result , every human person is my neighbor, and together we strive to more fully image the triune God. Practically, what does this mean for living human rights and solidarity? It is imperative to look at Catholic social teaching pragmatically within the context of social analysis. What would a program for human rights and solidarity as envisioned here require? Is it practically verifiable by those analyzing programs of human development? How would it differ from a purely secular approach to human rights and community?

3

Integral Human Development, Practicality, and Social Analysis

Development "is a process of expanding the real freedoms people enjoy."
Amartya Sen[1]

"To move forward constructively and fruitfully in the different functions and responsibilities involves the ability to analyze, understand, and engage . . . . serving the human family, especially the needy and those suffering from hunger and malnutrition."
Pope Francis, Address to the Food and Agriculture Organization[2]

Reflecting on Pope Paul VI's *Populorum Progressio*, Pope John Paul II contends: "the originality of the encyclical consists not so much in the affirmation, historical in character, of the universality of the social question but rather in the *moral evaluation* of this reality" (SRS 9), including the obligation to consider the social effects of development and poverty on the individual, national, and global levels. John Paul II goes on to explain Catholic social thought not as an alternative social theory but as a moral tradition (SRS 41). Chapter 2 offered systematic arguments for the philosophical and theological anthropological positions underpinning Catholic social thought's vision of human rights and solidarity. These anthropological positions lead to concrete ethical demands. Nominal assent to human rights and solidarity without a practical commitment to the necessary social matrix is empty. As a moral tradition, Catholic social teaching must dialogue with the social analysis of particular historical contexts.

---

1. Amartya Sen, *Development as Freedom* (New York: Anchor Books, 1999), 3.

2. Francis, "Address of His Holiness Pope Francis to Participants in the 38th Conference of the Food and Agriculture Organization of the United Nations (FAO)," June 20, 2013, http://en.radiovaticana.va/news/2013/06/20/pope_to_fao:_more_must_be_done_to_end_scandal_of_starvation/en1-703198.

An explicit example of this is Paul VI's own engagement with the emerging economic and political theories of development in *Populorum Progressio*. This dialogue with social science is an important response to those who would dismiss the vision of Catholic social thought as naive, overly optimistic, or disconnected from the actual realities of contemporary society. Nobel prize–winning Indian developmental economist Amartya Sen is currently a major architect of a renewed global focus on social and economic human rights and the importance of social structures. Through his many books and articles, most notably *Development as Freedom* (1999), Sen uses philosophy and economics to argue for particular understandings of freedom, human rights, and human capability within communities. This theory is foundational for global poverty efforts at the United Nations and United Nations Development Programme (UNDP), especially the emergence of the Millennium Development Goals (MDG) initiative.[3] Through dialogue with Sen, we can refine and challenge the vision of Catholic social thought and highlight the distinct contribution it makes to global human rights discourse.

Amartya Sen and Catholic social teaching do not share a theological anthropology or unified moral vision; however, he does represent a serious dialogue partner for engaging *all people of goodwill*. Despite being a self-proclaimed *nonreligious* person, Sen's work is deeply committed to taking seriously the religious and cultural commitments of individuals and communities as influential motivators for rational choice and action.[4] His work and influence provide both a theoretical interlocutor and, more importantly, practical analysis rooted in a holistic approach to human rights. By examining Sen's theory and the praxis of programs for the Millennium Development Goals, the need for Catholic social teaching's integrated approach and the value added to the analysis can be seen. First, through the exposition of substantive freedom and development, Sen's analysis confirms the need for an integrated and unified body of human rights, including the social and economic rights emphasized in Catholic social teaching. Using freedom as the frame, Sen demonstrates through concrete examples that all freedoms are interdependent and therefore all human rights are interdependent. Second, *Development as Freedom* provides analytical support for a connection between human rights and solidarity. Within this analysis is a realistic pragmatism, which is a helpful counterpart to the theoretical emphasis and optimism of Catholic social teaching and many human

---

3. United Nations, "United Nations Millennium Development Goals," http://www.un.org/millenniumgoals/.

4. Amartya Sen, *Development as Freedom* (New York: Anchor Books, 1999), 282–83.

rights approaches. Finally, given the limits of his focus on the individual and limited philosophical anthropology, Sen and the liberal tradition alone are insufficient to fully ground human rights and solidarity. Thus, Catholic social teaching adds something substantial to the boarder debate concerning both human rights and solidarity.

INTEGRATED HUMAN RIGHTS AND THE ANALYSIS OF DEVELOPMENT

For much of the last sixty years, development was simply equated with the growth of the gross national product (GNP) or individual incomes. *Populorum Progressio* argued against this narrow economic focus in favor of integral human development. Moreover, the extensive research by the United Nations Development Programme (UNDP) over the last twenty years has shown that economic growth does not automatically lead to greater human development within a nation or community.[5] Economic growth is merely one part of human development. Thus, Sen defines development more widely as "a process of expanding the real freedoms people enjoy."[6] Like Taylor, Sen develops a deeper and broader understanding of freedom. Increasing individual incomes, wealth, and GNP are important means for development; however, the true end of development is freedom: "if freedom is what development advances, then there is a major argument for concentrating on that overarching objective, rather than on some particular means, or some specially chosen list of instruments. Viewing development in terms of expanding substantive freedoms directs attention to the ends that make development important."[7] In a way that is similar to John Paul II and Benedict XVI's cautions about distorting the distinctions between means and ends concerning markets, Sen emphasizes purchasing power as a means and not the end of development. Thus, the building blocks for development are capabilities, freedom, and agency. Sen's expanded information base provides qualitative and quantitative support for integrated human rights, including civil, political, economic, and social rights as well as participative agency of persons realizing this freedom.[8]

Development as Freedom is primarily a *capability* theory of development, which evolved out of Sen's work in economics, on famines, and in collaboration with philosopher Martha Nussbaum. In "Capability and Well-Being," Sen

5. United Nations Development Programme (UNDP), "The Rise of the South: Human Progress in a Diverse World," Human Development Report 2013, http://www.undp.org/content/dam/undp/library/corporate/HDR/2013GlobalHDR/English/HDR2013 Report English.pdf.

6. Sen, *Development as Freedom*, 3.

7. Ibid., 3.

8. Ibid., 18.

admits "capability" appears to be an odd name but explains that the capability approach "is concerned with evaluating in terms of his or her actual ability to achieve various valuable functionings as part of living."[9] Therefore, "the capability approach can help to identify the possibility that two persons can have very different substantive opportunities even when they have the same set of means; for example: a disabled person can do far less than an able bodied person can with the exact same income and other 'primary goods.'"[10] Despite having the same economic means, they do not have the same opportunities. There are similarities here to Taylor's use of narrative identity, but, as an economist, Sen focuses more concretely on capabilities tied to available choices and opportunities versus developing a sense of freedom for (positive freedom), which for Sen is the freedom to achieve that which one chooses to value.

Through capabilities, Sen steers away from purely economic (GNP or income-centered) or legal approaches to human rights toward a broad understanding of freedoms that are both substantive and instrumental, capabilities or opportunities and process or agency. Human development and functioning as understood through capability "allows us to distinguish appropriately between (i) whether a person is actually able to do things she would value *doing*, and (ii) whether she possesses the *means* or *instruments or permissions* to pursue what she would like to do (her actual ability to do that pursuing may depend on many contingent circumstances)."[11] Sen argues the advantage of this approach, as social analysis, is the "evaluative focus" which includes both the "*realized functionings*" (actual choices an individual makes or has made) or the "*capability set of alternatives*" (those available opportunities). Adequate evaluation requires a broad information base and a clear distinguishing of types of freedom.[12] Avoiding starvation and participating in politics are both substantive freedoms. Throughout the corpus of his capabilities and development theory, Sen emphasizes the actual available opportunities from which a person can choose with respect to particular actions, values or lifestyles. In doing so, Sen prioritizes individual freedom and choice while acknowledging that agency is conditioned and limited by the conditions of one's social location.

9. Amartya Sen, "Capability and Well-Being," in *Quality of Life*, ed. Amartya Sen and Martha Nussbaum (Oxford: Oxford University Press, 1993), 30.

10. Amartya Sen, "Human Rights and Capabilities," *Journal of Human Devlopment* 6, no. 2 (July 2005): 154.

11. Ibid., 153. Cf. also Sen, *Development as Freedom*, 75.

12. Sen, *Inequality Reexamined* (Cambridge, MA: Harvard University Press, 1992), 117.

Therefore, agency grounds the philosophical concept of *substantive freedom*. Taking agency from philosophy and not economics, an agent is "someone who acts and brings about change, and whose achievements can be judged in terms of her own values and objectives" and is a "member of the public and . . . a participant in economic, political and social actions."[13] Substantive freedom, and by extension the freedom to achieve, is as much a matter of individual agency as the social support required to develop, placing a high value on human potentiality and prioritizing the potential values, lifestyles, and choices one may have reason to value. A crucial example of this is the role of education in expanding human rights and creating solidarity. A hallmark of the current global development agenda is the goal of universal primary education (Millennium Development Goal 2) by 2015. At once a poverty and human rights program, prioritizing access to primary education is a key instance of how individual agency and human rights cannot be separated from the need for adequate social structures and community. Universal primary education significantly enhances the capabilities of all in the community, expanding the common good, not just benefiting individuals. It is a part of the necessary social matrix.

Freedom is expanded well beyond simply freedom of choice or negative freedom. Sen offers a five-point definition of instrumental freedoms, delineating a clear set of variables from which to evaluate this substantive freedom to achieve: "(1) *political freedoms*, (2) *economic facilities*, (3) *social opportunities*, (4) *transparency guarantees* and (5) *protective security*. . . . Public policy to foster human capabilities and substantive freedoms in general can work through the promotion of these distinct yet interrelated instrumental freedoms."[14] *Political freedom* is largely self-explanatory and includes the basic civil and political rights "associated with democracies in the broadest sense," such as freedom of speech.[15] *Economic facilities* relates to the ability of the individual to access and participate in the labor market, "to utilize economic resources for the purpose of consumption, or production, or exchange."[16] Education and health care are perhaps the two most obvious and important examples of Sen's instrumental freedom category of *social opportunities*—arranged by society and without which we cannot effectively participate in the economic and political life of the community.[17] Education, and more simply the ability to read, is a significant

13. Sen, *Development as Freedom*, 19.
14. Ibid., 10.
15. Ibid., 38.
16. Ibid., 39.
17. Ibid.

precondition for achieving effective economic and political participation. If I cannot read, I cannot substantively exercise my human rights in community. The legal structure may offer me freedom of choice, but I do not have the substantive opportunity or capabilities to exercise these rights fully, and I do not have the same opportunity as those who are literate—even though we both have the same legal guarantees. Finally, *transparency guarantees* and *protective security* are interrelated instrumental freedoms that protect the legitimate functioning of interpersonal and societal relationships. Transparency guarantees, such as disclosure, highlight the need for trust in both interpersonal relations and the larger structural organization of society. If there is fear of widespread corruption, there can be no faith in the structures and economic space of the society, as the June 2013 protests against the Brazilian government's corruption illustrate. Similarly, protective security is necessary to deal with situations of extreme vulnerability.[18] All five of these instrumental freedoms are necessary for basic participation in community.

Freedom is both the principal means and end of development. Not only is Sen including the basic social and economic rights such as access to healthcare or education, he is also presenting the basic social conditions required for his understanding of human flourishing as the freedom to achieve, which is the end of development. Instrumental freedoms provide the means and substantive opportunity to achieve. As a group, they are the conditions necessary for the protection of basic human rights. For Sen, this participation is understood in terms of the substantive freedom to achieve what one chooses to value in life. It is quality not quantity of agency. While this is only part of the theology of participation in Catholic social teaching, it is an important step toward recognizing the importance of human participation. Impeding any one of these instrumental freedoms leads to widespread *unfreedom*, for Sen, Taylor, and Catholic social teaching. Sen emphatically argues, "Social arrangements may be decisively important in securing and expanding the freedom of the individual."[19] Through emphasizing that a lack of *economic facilities* is significant unfreedom, Sen provides a case not only for freedom as such but also for a unified understanding of human rights as inclusive of economic and social rights. Civil and political freedoms cannot be sacrificed, but alone they are not sufficient because they alone cannot achieve development.

---

18. Ibid., 40. Sen explains, "The domain of protective security includes *fixed* institutional arrangements such as unemployment benefits and statutory income supplements to the indigent as well as *ad hoc* arrangements such as famine relief or emergency public employment to generate income for destitutes."

19. Ibid., 42.

How does one evaluate whether or not development, in terms of expanding substantive freedoms, is occurring? How does one measure implementation of instrumental freedoms? As a social scientist, Sen deems this a matter of the necessary variables, such as *personal heterogeneities or environmental varieties*, which must be taken into consideration. The information set one is analyzing not only reveals one's operating presuppositions but also defines the possible solution set for a particular problem.[20] Thus, by having a complex information base, one avoids defining poverty and development solely in terms of income and income deprivation. In particular, "policy debates have indeed been distorted by overemphasis on income poverty and income inequality, to the neglect of deprivations that relate to other variables, such as unemployment, ill health, lack of education and social exclusion."[21] One clear example is the direct impact heating and medication costs have on a standard of living. In response, an integrated definition of poverty and corresponding policies must be developed.

The challenge of measuring poverty offers a lens into the differences between the capabilities approach and an income-dominated approach. Historically, poverty levels have been measured and defined almost entirely by reference to money—whether personal income or a nation's GNP/GDP

20. In *Development as Freedom*, Sen identifies five distinct sources that make up the information base and determine the correlation between one's annual income and the actual substantive freedom and well-being attained from that income and other resources. First, there are *personal heterogeneities*: "people have disparate physical characteristics connected with disability, illness, age or gender, and these make their needs diverse" (42). All of these differing physical attributes directly affect the resources necessary to enhance substantive freedom. Enhancing the substantive freedom of someone with physical disabilities requires greater economic and social resources than someone able-bodied. Second, there are *environmental diversities* due to climate, pollution, natural resources, and the like. The severity of one's climate, hot or cold, determines the level of heat and other such necessities required. Third, there are *variations in social climate* including education, access to health care, crime, and so on. These different variables are distinct, but related; for example, issues of pollution and infectious diseases are both environmental and social. Fourth, there are *differences in relational perspective*: "for example, being *relatively* poor in a rich community can prevent a person from achieving some elementary 'functionings' (such as taking part in the life of the community) even though her income, in absolute terms, may be much higher than the level of income at which members of poorer communities can function with great ease and success" (71). Finally, the last significant variable is *distribution within the family* in which "incomes earned by one or more family members are shared by all—non earners as well as earners. The family is thus the basic unit for consideration of incomes from the standpoint of their use. The well being or freedom of individuals in a family will depend on how the family income is used" (71). While in a single person family distribution is not a major factor, within families of two or more people distribution within the family will affect both the family and each individual's substantive freedoms.

21. Ibid., 108.

(gross domestic product). The global measure for extreme poverty is set at $1.25 per day. Since 1990, the United Nations Development Programme has sought a broader measure through the Human Development Index and yearly UNDP Human Development Reports. Most recently this has expanded into the development of the Multidimensional Poverty Index (MPI), developed in 2010 by Susan Alkire and Maria Santos at Oxford University's Oxford Poverty and Human Development Initiative.[22] Utilized in the 2010 Human Development Report, the MPI examines three key areas highlighted in Sen's capabilities theory: education, health, and living standards.[23] Used in companion with *money-based measures*, the MPI indicates that "about 1.7 billion people in 109 countries covered by the MPI . . . live in multidimensional poverty—that is, with at least 33 percent of the indicators reflecting acute deprivation in health, education, and standard of living. This exceeds the estimated 1.3 billion in those countries who live on $1.25 a day or less (though it is below the share who live on $2 or less)."[24] The MPI seeks to give a fuller picture of actual deprivation and poverty and also to measure the intensity and severity of those deprivations, including but not limited to income. For example, the MPI offers data concerning what extent of the poverty deprivation is due to health or education deprivation as well as income.

In evaluating development and freedom, one must take into account both the process and opportunity aspects of freedom and human rights. The social and economic rights highlighted in the multidimensional poverty index are largely a matter of substantive opportunities. From the perspective of Catholic social teaching, this is manifest in the centrality of judging from the margins and of the preferential option for the poor. If we are to say that all human persons have equal human dignity and thus are endowed with equal human rights, we must evaluate with respect to equality of opportunity for those on the margins. However, another important aspect of human rights is not properly a matter of capabilities but about freedom as process. To illustrate the difference, Sen offers the example of an adult woman, Natasha. Imagine Natasha has decided that she wants to go out this evening, and let us consider

22. Susan Alkire and Maria Santos "Acute Multidimensional Poverty: A new index for developing countries," *OPHI Working Paper 38*, UNDP HDRO Background Paper 2010/11 http://www.ophi.org.uk/wp-content/uploads/ophi-wp38.pdf (2013) "Measuring Acute Poverty in the Developing World: Robustness and Scope of the Multidimensional Poverty Index" OPHI Working Paper No 59. http://www.ophi.org.uk/wp-content/uploads/ophi-wp-59.pdf
23. "Multi-Dimensional Poverty Index," United Nations Development Programme, Human Development Reports, http://hdr.undp.org/en/statistics/mpi/.
24. "Multi-Dimensional Poverty Index."

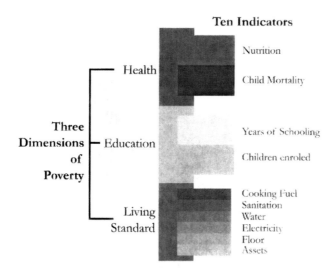

Figure 1: Alkire, S. and Santos, M. E. (2013) "Measuring Acute Poverty in the Developing World: Robustness and Scope of the Multidimensional Poverty Index". OPHI Working Paper No 59. http://www.ophi.org.uk/wp-content/uploads/ophi-wp-59.pdf. Used with Permission.

the ways in which her freedom can be violated with respect to this decision. First, her freedom can be violated by an authority barring her from going out (whether it be an authoritarian government or a household structure in which male permission is required for freedom of movement). Her freedom can also be violated, however, by her being forced to go out, even though she has herself decided to go out that evening.[25] Human flourishing as it relates to capabilities is a matter of "the opportunity to be able to have combinations of functionings (including in this case, the opportunity to be well-nourished), and the person is free to make use of this opportunity or not."[26] While Sen is critiqued for overreaching the concept of freedom, he responds by clarifying that it is "not being suggested at all that being well-nourished is to be seen as a freedom," but rather that the opportunity or capability to be well-nourished is a freedom.[27] The example of Natasha is important for Catholic social thought because it emphasizes why participation is a necessary condition for solidarity. If the development proposal or structure provides a basic good and is of benefit

25. Sen, "Human Rights and Capabilities," 153.

26. Ibid., 154.

27. Such as: Susan Moller Okin, "Poverty, Well-Being, and Gender: What Counts, Who's Heard?," *Philosophy & Public Affairs* 31, no. 3 (2003): 280–316. Sen, "Human Rights and Capabilities," 154.

but those affected are not involved and have no voice, have no participation or agency, it is not solidarity, just as it was not solidarity when Natasha had no voice in choosing her actions.

The interplay between opportunity and process is at the heart of why Sen does not offer one solution or argument for the one acceptable system of distribution, justice, or human development. It is also why, in recent years, Sen has become clearer that capability is a concept that is integral for the human rights project but that human rights are not all a matter of capabilities. Moving beyond simply capability, the process aspect of freedom and human rights revolves around the recognition of two key aspects of human agency. First, the freedom–oriented approach prioritizes individual agency in such a way that people "cannot be seen merely as patients to whom the benefits will be dispensed by the process of development," while at the same time recognizing the real pragmatic importance of the necessary social structures.[28] Second, participation and the deliberation of public reasoning is crucial to the establishment of human rights: "Indeed, the freedom to participate in critical evaluation and in the process of value formation is among the most crucial freedoms of social existence."[29] Lack of proper education, as noted earlier, represents significant unfreedom not only as it pertains to social and political participation but also with respect to communication, as evidenced in the exposition of language in the previous chapter.

Major components of the social support necessary are public goods, which are those goods that, if they exist, are present for all, such as a system of traffic lights. A system of traffic lights and infrastructure exist for all members of the community. Sen contends that public health should be understood within the framework of public goods. For example, a social program for eradicating malaria is a public good, not a private one, even if it is due to the actions of an individual: "I may be willing to pay my share in a social program of malaria eradication, but I cannot buy my part of that protection in the form of a 'private good' (like an apple or a shirt). It is a 'public good'—malaria-free surroundings—which we have to consume together. Indeed, if I do manage to organize a malaria-free environment where I live, my neighbor too will have that . . . without having to 'buy' it from anywhere."[30] These public or *semipublic* goods require "social provisioning that arises from the need of basic capabilities, such as elementary health care and basic educational opportunities"[31] and cannot

28. Sen, *Development as Freedom*, 288.
29. Ibid., 287.
30. Ibid, 128.
31. Ibid.

simply rest on market mechanisms of development. Within the international community this approach has been gaining ground as the deep impact of public health is broadened well beyond the context of epidemics. In the Millennium Declaration of 2002, 189 countries pledged a commitment to radically reduce extreme poverty and deprivation. As the 2003 UNDP Human Development Report states, "The Millennium Development Goals address many of the most enduring failures of human development. Unlike the objectives of the first, second and third UN Development Decades (1960s, 1970s, 1980s), which mostly focused on economic growth, the Goals place human well-being and poverty reduction at the centre of global development objectives."[32] The eight Millennium Development Goals are as follows:

1. Eradicate extreme poverty and hunger
2. Achieve universal primary education
3. Promote gender equality and empower women
4. Reduce child mortality
5. Improve maternal health
6. Combat HIV/AIDS, malaria and other diseases
7. Ensure environmental sustainability
8. Develop a global partnership for development[33]

Examined together, the Multidimensional Poverty Index and the Millennium Development Goals offer measures that concretize and can be used to assess integral human development as it is understood in Catholic social thought. On the one hand, the MPI shows that more people are living in serious deprivation than just those below the $1.25 per day global poverty line. At the same time, the multidimensional approach shows that human development gains are occurring through social policy, as evidenced, for example, by Mexico's attention to public health.[34]

> Mexico. In 2003, the Mexican state approved Seguro Popular, a public insurance scheme that provides access to comprehensive health care for poor households formerly excluded from traditional social security. Public resources for health have increased and are being distributed more fairly. Access to and use of health care services have expanded. Financial

32. United Nations Development Programme (UNDP), "Human development Report 2003," 27, http://hdr.undp.org/sites/default/files/reports/264/hdr_2003_en_complete.pdf.
33. UN, "United Nations Millennium Development Goals."
34. UNDP, "Rise of the South," 81.

protection indicators have improved. By the end of 2007, 20 million poor
people were benefiting from the scheme. Mexico is a leader in moving
rapidly towards universal health coverage by adopting an innovative
financing mechanism. (UNDP Human Development Report 2013, p. 81.)

The success of this program in Mexico led to a pilot study in New
York City (2007–2010).[35] New York City, which had already moved to its
own supplemental poverty measure, found mixed results. The program did
successfully lift the participants above the poverty line, impacting aspects of
material poverty such as food insecurity; however, as both participants and the
control group already had relatively high school attendance as well as access
to extensive preexisting programs to provide health care within New York
State, the impact on those areas was limited.[36] The need for multidimensional
approaches focused on expanding capabilities applies to both the developed
and developing world; however, the particular needs of the individual context
will dictate differences in programs and emphasis. Yet, the holistic impact of
programs tends to expand beyond the immediate investment in education and
health care to ripple out in civil society. For example, increasing mother's
access to education significantly increases the survival of children under five
years old.[37] This is why Catholic social thought insists on integral human
development as the center of any development agenda. Integral human
development and the multidimensional approach are demonstrated to be
effective.

As the UNDP 2013 Human Development Report notes, "pro-poor policies
and significant investments in people's capabilities—through a focus on
education, nutrition and health, and employment skills—can expand access to
decent work and provide for sustained progress."[38] As a result of this concerted
effort, the UNDP notes that "no country had a lower HDI [human

35. Ibid., 85. See also "Opportunity NYC: Family Rewards," http://www.nyc.gov/html/ceo/
downloads/pdf/ceo_report_family_rewards_pdf

36. Julie Bosman, "City Will Stop Paying the Poor for Good Behavior," *New York Times*, March 30,
2010,http://www.nytimes.com/2010/03/31/nyregion/31cash.html?_r=0.

37. United Nations Development Programme (UNDP), *The Millennium Development Goals Report
2012* (New York: United Nations, 2012), 28, http://www.un.org/millenniumgoals/pdf/MDG Report
2012.pdf.

38. United Nations Development Programme (UNDP), "Human Development Report 2013
Summary," ii, http://hdr.undp.org/en/media/HDR2013_EN_Summary.pdf.

development index] value in 2012 than in 2000, in contrast to the prior decade, when 18 countries had a lower HDI value in 2000 than in 1990."[39]

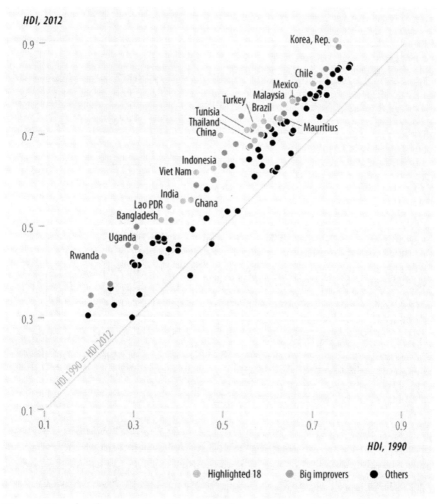

Figure 2. More than forty countries of the South had greater gains on the human development index (HDI) between 1990 and 2012 than would have been predicted from their previous performance on the HDI. UNDP, "Human Development Report 2013 Summary." "Note: Countries above the 45 degree line had a higher HDI value in 2012 than in 1990. Blue and grey markers indicate countries with significantly larger than predicted increases in HDI value between 1990 and 2012 given their HDI value in 1990. These countries were identified based on residuals obtained from a regression of the change in log of HDI between 2012 and 1990 on the log of HDI in 1990. Source: HDRO calculations."

39. UNDP, "Rise of the South," 12.

Through this focus on freedom as the means and end of development, the interdependence of both political and economic freedoms becomes evident. Practically, this has been enacted by the United Nations over the last fifteen years. The results provide analytical support for a connection between the community, human rights, and the struggle to achieve solidarity. One example of expanding capabilities and increasing human development noted above is Ghana.[40] According to Ghana's Millennium Development Goal reports of 2006 and 2010, the government made strategic investments in social structures—namely, improving primary education—arguing that it viewed "basic education as a fundamental building block of the economy" long before the Millennium Declaration.[41]

"One of the earliest initiatives in independent Ghana was the 1951 Accelerated Development Plan for Education, which aimed at a massive expansion of primary and middle school education. The 1961 Education Act removed fees for elementary education so that households had to pay only a modest amount for textbooks. Enrolment in public elementary schools doubled over the next six years. Between 1966 and 1970, the public discourse on education moved from access to quality. In the early 1970s, the focus came back to access, this time for secondary education. The next major round of reforms took place in 1987. The most significant aspect of the curriculum reform was to provide children with literacy in three languages—two Ghanaian languages and English—as well as modern farming skills, vocational skills and practical mathematics skills" (UNDP Human Development Report 2013, p. 78.)

Through the national MDG reports, Ghana's government identified strategies to achieve and progress toward the MDGs. Ghana demonstrated an integrated approach to education through policies on infrastructure, school food programs, free uniforms and books, and a strong national effort to deploy forty thousand volunteers as well as twenty thousand more recruits.[42] This focus on expanding basic human rights has a demonstrated effect on human development, which reverberates beyond education. Furthermore, the multidimensional approach positively impacts economic growth. A focus on expanding capabilities is clear,

40. UNDP, "Rise of the South," 79.

41. "Ghana Millennium Development Goals, 2006 Report," 12, http://www.undp.org/content/dam/undp/library/MDG/english/MDG Country Reports/Ghana/MDG Report 2006 Ghana.pdf.

42. "2010 Ghana Millennium Development Goals Report," submitted November 2012, 26, http://www.ndpc.gov.gh/GPRS/2010 Ghana's MDGs Report (Final) - Nov2012.pdf.

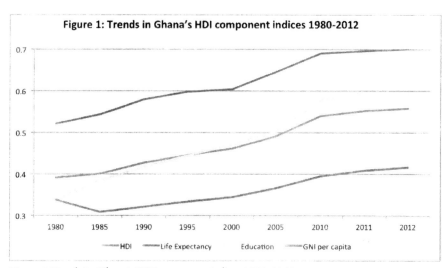

Figure 3. Trends in Ghana's HDI component indices 1980-2012

as is the interdependence of the MDGs. In particular, programs related to safe motherhood and child health are referenced throughout—it is difficult to isolate any of the MDGs from the others. In both the 2006 and 2010 reports, the struggle for gender parity in education and gender equality persists. Investments in infrastructure and programs must be matched by community building beyond creating the structures for individual capabilities and freedom.

Recognizing the centrality of social opportunities to support individual agency, Sen states, "Individuals live and operate in a world of institutions. Our opportunities and prospects depend crucially on what institutions exist and how they function. Not only do institutions contribute to our freedoms, their roles can be sensibly evaluated in light of their contributions to our freedom."[43] For this reason, UNDP calls for a focus on developing social institutions and strengthening transparency. Moreover, in the 2012 Millennium Development Goals Report, the UNDP notes achievements in lowering extreme poverty and reducing malaria deaths as examples of integrated human rights for individuals and communities, and it also recognizes that sluggish progress toward gender equality is a barrier to human rights..[44] This demonstrates the need for a broader social matrix of human rights and solidary, more than just institutions and policies. Combating the sluggish progress on gender equality requires

43. Sen, *Development as Freedom*, 142.
44. UNDP, *Millennium Development Goals Report 2012*.

both targeted policies as well as greater attention to equality, mutuality, and reciprocity in the community, as highlighted in the previous chapter.

THE PRAXIS OF CONNECTING HUMAN RIGHTS AND SOLIDARITY AND PRAGMATIC CAUTIONS

The right to development was highlighted in the first chapter as perhaps the clearest indication of the Catholic approach to human rights and its understanding of the role of the community. As I stated, this human right was recognized in Catholic social teaching long before it was officially added to the United Nations canon. Sen's framework develops this understanding of development as a human right in practice. This dialogue with social science and the practical human rights agenda offers data to support a broader approach. The social sciences and Sen, in particular, also provide a necessary caution concerning available resources. What does one do when there are not sufficient resources for the comprehensive human rights agenda? How does one prioritize? Sen offers helpful parameters for the question of limited resources; however, beyond this, he does not offer a comprehensive understanding of the community or solidarity. The closest Sen gets is his recognition that "as reflective creatures we have the ability to contemplate the lives of others. . . . It is not so much a matter of having exact rules about how precisely we ought to behave, as of recognizing the relevance of our shared humanity in making the choices we face."[45] What emerges from dialogue is practical success in expanding human rights and development through a broader approach, a helpful as well as necessary caution concerning available resources, and solidarity as the crucial addition Catholic social teaching brings to the global conversation.

One of the important insights from Sen for Catholic social thought is a caution against neglecting practical implementation questions regarding human rights. This caution is important for all who seek to expand human rights. The project or processes of development and human rights require evaluating the distribution of resources with sometimes difficult choices. In particular, there are many complexities with enhancing social and economic human rights that cannot be solved merely by recognizing their status as human rights. Within most developing countries, Sen points out, discussions of programs for social and economic rights often include questioning people's demonstrated need and ability to pay for services when prioritizing government resources "even for free medical care and health services, or free educational

45. Sen, *Development as Freedom*, 283.

facilities."[46] Despite his commitment to human rights and endorsement of social and economic rights, Sen also admits the validity and appropriateness of these questions of need and ability to pay within developing countries that have limited resources.[47]

Practically, this is why the lessons and data in the UNDP reports are crucial for enhancing human rights and development—they help communities make evidence-based decisions on limited resources. Arguing against those who say basic social protections are simply too expensive, the UNDP data shows that in the long term these investments bear fruit and that basic human rights can be secured through public and private investment. These basic social provisions are inalienable rights of persons, and it is imperative that these ethical demands be enacted such that persons have substantive exercise of these rights.

Admitting a pre-economic social principle, in which universal economic and social rights are posited regardless of particular economic resources to guarantee said rights, is an important step. "Human rights include significant and influenceable economic and social freedoms. . . . The current unrealizability of any accepted human right, which can be promoted through institutional or political change, does not, by itself, convert that claim to a *non*-right."[48] Human rights are primarily ethical demands, which require more than simply legal recognition or legal structures to be exercised. This is perhaps most clearly seen in the sluggish progress on the MDGs concerning women's equality. The 2012 MDG Report acknowledges that "Gender inequality persists and women continue to face discrimination in access to education, work and economic assets, and participation in government. Violence against women continues to undermine efforts to reach all goals. Further progress to 2015 and beyond will largely depend on success on these interrelated challenges."[49] Gender equality is one example where the ethical demands of human rights require an entire culture to be accomplished, including legal recognition, social structures, and a stronger understanding of the community. Human rights need social structures, but they are also intimately linked to the integrity of the community. According to the UNDP Human Development Report 2013, which focused

---

46. Ibid., 130.

47. Sen addresses and refutes the main arguments for denying economic and social rights, or second-generation human rights. He reiterates that both civil-political and socioeconomic rights place obligations and duties on us and require social structures in order to be realized. Cf. Amartya Sen, "Elements of a Human Rights Theory," *Philosophy & Public Affairs* 32, no. 4 (Autumn 2004): 315–56. Sen, *Development as Freedom*, 131.

48. Sen, "Elements of a Human Rights Theory," 320.

49. UNDP, *Millennium Development Goals Report 2012*, 5.

on the global South, "education, health care, social protections, legal empowerment, and social organization all enable poor people to participate in growth. But even these basic policy instruments may not empower disenfranchised groups" on the margins because lack of "local institutional capacity and community involvement" provide added barriers for participation, particularly for gender equality. [50] Yet, there has been some significant progress.

> Achieving parity in education is an important step toward equal opportunity for men and women in the social, political and economic domains. Driven by national and international efforts and the MDG campaign, many more of the world's children have enrolled in school at the primary level, especially since 2000. Girls have benefited the most. Progress is reflected in the gender parity index (GPI), showing the ratio between the enrolment rate of girls and that of boys. The GPI grew from 91 in 1999 to 97 in 2010 for the developing regions as a whole.[51]

Building on this success and overcoming broader discrimination is a matter of both policies and deeper understanding of the person and community. If secondary school is available for girls, will families allow and promote their education? In families and countries with limited resources, who determines who gains access to education? These pragmatic concerns are often eschewed by the invocation of human rights; however, they are real and must be addressed if we are to achieve the goal of human development and unmask discrimination to make solidarity possible, as we will examine in the next chapter.

One's conception of the human person and of the theoretical grounding of human rights is crucial if the human rights project is to succeed, if *substantive freedom* is to be enhanced. It is important, however, to also engage the complexities and compromises of the contemporary social, economic, and political world. In Christian ethics, the reality of sin, both personal and social, acts as a caution against a naive or unchecked optimism in practice. For social ethics, Sen offers both a strong commitment to human rights as well as a realistic appraisal of distributing limited resources and the step-by-step process by which development occurs. Sen reminds us that the theory and justification of human rights as well as a pragmatic implementation of human rights policies and programs are necessary. In response to those who would dismiss an approach

50. UNDP, "Rise of the South," 78.
51. UNDP, *Millennium Development Goals Report 2012*, 2.

as unrealistic, he also provides social-scientific evidence that social structures, social and economic rights, and a broader role for the community in human rights are practical and necessary.

Value Added: A Fuller Understanding of the Common Good

If substantive freedom and development are to be understood within the context of human rights, "it is critically important to see the relationship between the force and appeal of human rights, on the one hand, and their reasoned justification and scrutinized use on the other."[52] In "Elements of a Human Rights Theory," Sen argues that the project of human rights requires an adequate theory grounding these rights and provides the basic elements for his own human rights theory. Catholic social thought locates the foundation for human rights in the view of the human person and community. In contrast, Sen introduces a secular human rights theory that deals with both ethical distinctions through use of Kantian philosophy and Adam Smith's economics. In order to protect the primacy of the freedom to achieve and the diversity of cultures, Sen makes almost no anthropological claims beyond the freedom to choose and the ability to offer reasons for one's choices and values. From this, "Human rights generate reasons for action for agents who are in a position to help in the promoting or safeguarding of the underlying freedoms. The induced obligations primarily involve the duty to give reasonable consideration to the reasons for action and their practical implications, taking into account the relevant parameters of the individual case."[53] Thus, in developing his human rights theory without strong anthropological claims, community is relegated to an instrumental role. As such, *development as freedom* is insufficient for a full understanding of the relationship between human rights and solidarity. Here the vision of Catholic social thought can add substance to the analysis of the human rights and development project.

Hesitating to make sweeping claims of objectivity and universality, Sen does attack those who claim that human rights are merely a Western construct contrary to "Asian values." There is, Sen admits, something extremely appealing about a set of human rights that apply to all peoples, regardless of culture, location, and such. In order for a theory of human rights to be successful, however, those rights must refer to something about the human person—freedom. He explains, "By starting from the importance of freedoms as the appropriate human condition on which to concentrate . . . we get a

---

52. Sen, "Elements of a Human Rights Theory," 317.
53. Ibid., 319.

motivating reason not only for celebrating our own rights and liberties, but also for our taking an interest in the significant freedoms of others."[54] Therefore, freedom is the central anthropological claim grounding human rights as well as one of the threshold conditions required for their exercise. And, it is the one clear anthropological claim made throughout Sen's writings on human rights.

To illustrate his point, Sen posits a story, similar to that of Natasha, of an Indian woman named Rima. He then considers two cases: one in which Rima decides she would like to go out for the evening and another in which she is either forced to stay home or forced to go out against her will. In being forced against her will, Sen explains that "Rima loses freedom in two different ways, related respectively to (1) being forced with no freedom of choice, and (2) being obliged in particular to do something she would not choose to do."[55] Once again, Sen argues that capabilities and substantive freedom are broad enough to address the complexities of the opportunity aspect of freedom while still maintaining the important process aspects as well. Freedom as the descriptive characteristic of the human person, then, "allows us to distinguish appropriately between (1) what she values *doing* or *being*, and (2) the *means* she has to achieve what she values," while taking into consideration all the contingencies of one's individual ability or disability.[56] Herein lies the foundation for human rights and the concern for others' rights.

Despite extensive attention to freedom and, in particular, the categories of substantive freedom and capabilities, Sen does not offer any stronger or more specific anthropological claims. Unlike Taylor, he does not focus on the communal nature of agency or the process of developing freedom. While Sen prioritizes the social conditions necessary for the individual to develop as an agent, the substantive opportunities necessary for a particular capability to be exercised, one does not get a clear sense of who this human person is to whom human rights are ascribed. In a manner similar to his arguments against those who reject human rights as anti-Asian, Sen expressly avoids detailed and universal anthropological claims of the human person or the person's identity in relation to the community; instead, he argues that "making sense of identity" remains a matter of personal choice and freedom. A limited anthropology, in Sen's framework, provides the space for diverse identities and communities.[57]

54. Ibid., 328.

55. Ibid., 331. This violation of freedom is present even if she is forced to do that which she would have freely chosen.

56. Ibid., 332.

57. Amartya Sen, *Identity and Violence: The Illusion of Destiny* (New York: Norton, 2006), 18–39. This focus on diversity and personal choice, for Sen, is the way to avoid identity-based violence.

However, the individual person's relationship to others remains vague. He emphatically argues for participation in decision making, democratic practices, and public reasoning; however, the focus is always on the individual engaging in or benefiting from the social. Despite acknowledging that human beings are social creatures and that enhancing substantive freedom requires both social structures and community, universality appears limited to choice and the community is seen simply as instrumental.

Substantive freedom recognizes the need for community and that without social opportunities, individual agency is limited—the absence of social structures represents significant unfreedom. The focus, however, is always on the individual. Furthermore, Sen acknowledges the needed balance between individual and social responsibility: "without the substantive freedom and capability to do something a person cannot be responsible for doing it. But actually having the freedom and capability to do something does impose on the person the *duty to consider* whether to do it or not, and this does involve individual responsibility."[58] The duty to consider, in Sen's thought, is the correlative to human rights. This means that if one has a right to life, then one has the duty to consider living it becomingly, to use the language of *Pacem in Terris* as a reference point. In the duty to consider, both the similarities to and differences from Catholic social teaching become clear. Where *Pacem in Terris* states that the right to life includes a duty to live that life becomingly, Sen argues the duty implicit in the right is to consider living it becomingly. The difference in the obligation here is crucial for Catholic social thought's understanding of the community and solidarity.

The distinctions illustrated by the duty to consider become clearer in "Elements of a Human Rights Theory," in which Sen explains the obligations associated with human rights. He relies on a distinction between perfect and imperfect duties from Immanuel Kant.[59]

> Human rights generate reasons for action for agents who are in a position to help in the promoting or safeguarding of the underlying freedoms. The induced obligations primarily involve the duty to give reasonable consideration to the reasons for action and their practical implications, taking into account the relevant parameters of the individual case. The reasons for action can support both "perfect" obligations as well as "imperfect" ones, which are less precisely

---

58. Sen, *Development as Freedom*, 284.

59. Immanuel Kant, *Grounding for the Metaphysics of Morals*, trans. James W. Ellington (Cambridge, MA: Hackett, 1993), loc. 540, 543.

characterized. Even though they differ in content, imperfect obligations are correlative with human rights in much the same way as perfect obligations. In particular, the acceptance of imperfect obligations goes beyond volunteered charity or elective virtues.[60]

In Sen's use of Kant, perfect obligations involve the individual person's direct agency and a negative duty not to violate another. Perfect obligations are universal and negative in nature. As the primary actor, each individual person has a "perfect obligation" not to violate another person's human rights. For example, if it is my human right to not be persecuted for my beliefs, as in freedom of thought or freedom of religion, then others have a perfect obligation not to persecute me for my beliefs. Since these are negative and universal in nature, there is no perfect obligation to live life becomingly that corresponds to the right to life with reference to my own human rights. Imperfect obligations, on the other hand, emerge when one is only secondarily related to the violation or deprivation in question. These are positive in scope and do not translate into a universal principle. Torture or, more specifically, the right not to be tortured is another clear example Sen uses to illustrate this distinction. For example, while I have a perfect obligation not to torture someone else, I have an imperfect obligation to intervene to stop torture inflicted by a third party. Since I am not the primary actor, any obligation is "imperfect."

What, then, is one's imperfect obligation? What is my obligation to intervene to stop others from being persecuted for their religion, race, class, and so forth? According to Sen, in the face of deprivation and human rights violations, one has an imperfect obligation to give "reasonable consideration" to action and intervention.[61] He is moving from a violation of human rights based on the general importance of freedom to an obligation to reasonably or seriously consider action or intervention, but this obligation does not mandate action or intervention. In fact, Sen specifically states that one does not have an obligation to intervene to stop or prevent every human rights violation—such a moral prescription would be paralyzing for an individual. As Sen explains, "The duty of reasonable consideration will not, in a great many cases, translate into an obligation to take on an elaborate scrutiny—only a willingness to do just that, when it seems relevant and appropriate."[62] For example, a moral

60. Sen, "Elements of a Human Rights Theory," 319.
61. Ibid., 339. He explains, "Even though the acknowledgement that certain freedoms qualify as human rights already reflects an assessment of their general importance . . . a person has to go beyond these pervasive features into more specific circumstances in giving reasonable consideration to what he or she, in particular, should do in a specific case."

obligation to act would not make sense in a situation where it is impossible or implausible that action will have the desired effect of enhancing substantive freedoms and promoting human rights. One must also be wary of interventions that may cause harm, despite good intentions. It is imperative, in the process of reasonable consideration, to determine whether or not one is in a position to help or make a difference.

To illustrate the distinctions of imperfect obligations, Sen uses the often-cited example of the 1964 murder of Kitty Genovese in Kew Gardens, Queens, who was brutally attacked and murdered on the street while neighbors watched from safely inside their apartments, doing nothing.[63] Those watching this horrific crime did not intervene, did not even call the police. In this situation, the perpetrator violated his "perfect obligation" not to assault and murder this young woman; "the others who did nothing whatever to help the victim also transgressed their general—and 'imperfect'—obligation to seriously consider providing the help which they could reasonably be expected to provide."[64] The distinction between perfect and imperfect obligations is important in evaluating the ethics of human rights practice and the obligations of solidarity. As will be addressed in detail in the final chapter, the relationship between human rights and solidarity falls within this broad category of imperfect obligations, in which the complexities of multiple actors and contingent factors (such as ability to help, risk to oneself, and the like) require serious consideration before the ethical action can be determined. Catholic social teaching, with its commitment to both human rights and solidarity, however, goes beyond an obligation to seriously consider action on another's behalf. While accounts of what actually occurred in 1964 are disputed, the case has become a landmark example for examining bystander responsibility, psychology, and moral obligations regarding intervention. For instance, John G. Simon, Charles W. Powers, and Jon P. Gunnemann developed the five Key Gardens Principles, in which there is a positive moral duty to help when there is (1) need, a person or persons in critical need; (2) proximity, one is sufficiently near the person to be aware of the need; (3) ability, one is actually capable of assisting; (4) last resort; and (5) no undue loss, those providing aid will not suffer loss disproportionate to the good provided by assisting.[65] These principles are an important step in moving

---

62. Ibid., 340.

63. Learning Network, "March 13, 1964 | New York Woman Killed While Witnesses Do Nothing," *New York Times*, March 13, 2012, http://learning.blogs.nytimes.com/2012/03/13/march-13-1964-new-york-woman-killed-while-witnesses-do-nothing/.

64. Sen, "Elements of a Human Rights Theory," 341.

from an imperfect obligation to seriously consider action to a responsibility to protect.

Imperfect moral obligations are not based only on universal principles but require a highly contextualized moral analysis of one's obligation using moral principles. In the end, Catholic social thought moves beyond the Kew Gardens principles and argues for concrete moral obligations resulting from moral analysis. Where Sen relies on Kant for a foundation, Catholic social thought builds on the philosophy of Thomas Aquinas. For Aquinas, morality is both objective and circumstantial. Any specific human action is either morally good or morally bad; yet, as Brian Davies, OP, notes, "hard and fast rules are none too easily available as yardsticks against which to measure the rightness or wrongness of particular actions in precise situations."[66] There are universal prohibitions, such as those against torture or killing the innocent; however, human action itself requires practical reasoning about the nature of the act, intention, and circumstances. In short, it requires moral analysis such as Sen's "rational consideration." Yet, for Aquinas, at the end of that moral analysis one's decision is concretely morally right or wrong.[67] Therefore, Catholic social thought begins with an understanding of imperfect obligations that incorporates objective morality and attention to the radical particularity of a particular situation. In Catholic social thought, discernment and the virtue of prudence do not establish a universal perfect obligation as the primary criterion for a moral obligation to act. Moral obligations to promote human rights or to act when the rights of others are being violated are imperfect obligations, but for Catholic social thought that failure to act, not just the failure to consider action, can be a moral failure. Sen's unwillingness to move from an obligation to seriously consider to more robust obligation to act significantly limits a comprehensive understanding of the human person as the foundation for human rights and solidarity.

65. John G. Simon, Charles W. Powers, and Jon P. Gunnemann, "The Responsibilities of Corporations and Their Owners," in *The Ethical Investor: Universities and Corporate Responsibility* (New Haven, CT: Yale University Press, 1972).

66. Thomas Aquinas distinguishes between human actions involving reason and will and *acts of a human being*, which are involuntary or reflexive. A summary of this position can be found in: Brian Davies, OP, *The Thought of Thomas Aquinas* (Oxford: Clarendon, 1992), 237.

67. While I do not have the space to detail Aquinas's theory of human action here, for more information see St. Thomas Aquinas, *Summa Theologica*, trans. Fathers of the English Dominican Province (Allen, TX: Christian Classics, 1991), vol. 2: Ia–IIae, Questions 18–21; and Davies, *Thought of Thomas Aquinas*.

Sen's ambiguity on the social aspects of a philosophy of the person has been highlighted in contrast to Taylor's perspective or Catholic social thought. Sen's focus on personal freedom is further emphasized in his examination of the self in economic theory. In *Rationality and Freedom*, Sen examines "four features of the self": self-centered welfare, self-welfare goal, self-goal choice, and self-assessment/reasoning. He defines the first three as those present in traditional models of rational behavior as the pursuit of self-interest: "1. *Self-centered welfare:* a person's welfare depends only on her own consumption and other features of the richness of her life (without any sympathy or antipathy towards others, and without procedural concern). 2. *Self-welfare goal:* a person's only goal is to maximize her own welfare. 3. *Self-goal choice:* a person's choices must be based entirely on the pursuit of her own goals."[68] All of these are prioritized in mainstream neoclassical economic theory; however, "a person is not only an entity that can enjoy one's own consumption, experience and appreciate one's welfare, and have goals but also an entity that can examine one's values and objectives and choose in light of those values."[69] Thus, he argues for the inclusion of self-assessment and reasoning in which "this broader framework can allow the acknowledgment of goals that are not exclusively reduced to one's own welfare and the recognition of values of appropriate social behavior for example, given the understanding of the goals of others living in society."[70]

Throughout his economics, Sen provides clear arguments for the inclusion of obligations toward other people and provides evidence and justification for the rationality of motivations outside self-interest: "we need to depart both from the assumption of given preferences (as in traditional social choice theory) and from the presumption that people are narrowly self-interested *homo economicus* (as in traditional public choice theory)."[71] It is rational and easily verifiable that individuals make choices based on motivations other than self-interest; Sen wants to recognize the importance of family, culture, and education. Specifically arguing for the rationality or *reasonableness* of these concerns, Sen states, "A person may have reason not to pursue her own goals relentlessly when this makes it hard for others to pursue their goals. This type of reasoning (related to going beyond the limits of 'self-goal choice') has a 'social' basis which both Immanuel Kant (1788) and Adam Smith (1790) have extensively

---

68. Amartya Sen, "Introduction: Rationality and Freedom," in *Rationality and Freedom* (Cambridge, MA: Belknap, 2004), 33–34.

69. Ibid., 36.

70. Ibid., 36.

71. Sen, "Rationality and Social Choice," in *Rationality and Freedom*, 289.

discussed," as has John Rawls.[72] However, in his arguments for the social nature, Sen does not attack the rationality of the self-interested model of humanity itself. While he argues for a broader knowledge base in his *Idea of Justice* and for a rational basis for interests not based on self-interest, he does not fault the neoclassical economic model of *homo economicus* itself as invalid.[73] Instead, he argues for expanding the possibility interests and motivations that are rational. Furthermore, the identity or value of community as such remains ancillary to the definition of the human person. The extent of the claim Sen makes in relation to motivation and values based on the welfare and values of others is limited to the argument that these are not irrational. He does not take the next step and question, either theoretically or empirically, the basic rationality or legitimacy of the *homo economicus* model. However, while Catholic social teaching agrees on the need for a broader information base, it does not accept isolated self-interested motivation as simply one legitimate option among many. For Catholic social thought, as Pope Francis explains, "self-knowledge is only possible when we share in a greater memory" (LF 38).

The purpose of returning once again to Sen's conception of the person and his anthropological claims is to illustrate two key elements that provide useful insights and demonstrate his limitations in connection with Catholic social teaching. First, all of the works referenced here are part of a long intellectual argument made by Sen for broadening the conception of rationality and freedom that has dominated traditional post-Enlightenment economic theory. Through his insistence of self-assessing reasoning, as well as the technical arguments concerning social-choice theory and welfare economics, Sen offers philosophical and social economic analysis that seeks to faithfully examine reality and promote substantive freedom. Human persons are always embedded in a social matrix. Their choices are always conditioned and constrained, and, as a result, despite his strong commitment to social and economic opportunities, Sen's conception of the community remains purely functional. Community is necessary for the development of the individual. The enhancement of the substantive freedom of persons requires an extensive list of social and economic opportunities but also the social milieu for these to flourish. For example, the substantive freedom of women depends not only on availability of education and health care but also a culture that promotes their full equality. And yet, despite clear support for community and the sociality of the human person, the community remains purely instrumental. The group

72. Sen, "Introduction: Rationality and Freedom," 41.

73. Amartya Sen, *The Idea of Justice* (Cambridge, MA: Harvard University Press, 2009).

or society certainly has a profound influence on the individual, but this does not appear to be more than an observable reality. Solidarity and the common good in Catholic social thought recognizes that the community is not just instrumentally necessary for the individual. There is integrity to the community itself.

Despite Sen's deep and abiding commitment to freedom and human rights, the imperfect obligation to seriously consider action on behalf of others never reaches the force of Taylor's obligation to belong.[74] One does not get the sense of a communal agency or identity that is positive and not simply functional. The philosophy of the person and community detailed in chapter 2 involves a sense of individual and communal identity in which the community is a constitutive element of developing one's individual agency and identity, and not merely a functional space in which the individual develops. There is a clear difference between Sen's assertion that substantive freedom and capabilities impose "on the person the duty to consider whether to do it or not" and Taylor's argument that prioritizing substantive freedom means "I ought to become the kind of agent who is capable of authentic conviction . . . that I ought to in certain circumstances to help foster this capacity in others, that I ought to bring up my children to have it."[75] Moreover, Taylor's inclusion of a responsibility to and for future generations is not evident in Sen's thought. Here Catholic social teaching offers a distinct contribution to the broader conversation on human rights.

CONCLUSION

Amartya Sen is a developmental economist, and as a social scientist his focus is on empirically verifiable social analysis. As such, his groundbreaking work on famines led him to further investigate theories of development and welfare economics, ultimately in the service of a commitment to human rights. Throughout this chapter, Sen's work has been invoked to illustrate that Catholic social teaching's vision of human rights as a unified body, including economic and social rights, can be confirmed through social analysis. Furthermore, in arguing for the economic and social opportunities necessary for substantive freedom, Sen's *Development as Freedom* provides analytical support for a necessary connection between human rights and solidarity. In order for the insights of Catholic social teaching to be relevant to the development of human

74. Cf. Charles Taylor, "Atomism," in *Philosophical Papers*, vol. 2: *Philosophy and the Human Sciences* (Cambridge: Cambridge University Press, 1985), 206.

75. Sen, *Development as Freedom*, 284. Taylor, "Atomism," 194.

rights policy and practice, there must be a connection with the practical evaluation of social science on the ground. Sen's exposition, therefore, provides ammunition against those who charge that the vision of human rights offered in *Pacem in Terris* is naive and unrealistically optimistic. A holistic approach to human rights through substantive freedom, including all five instrumental freedoms, is the only program by which one can implement human rights in such a way as to enhance the real capabilities of persons. Given his minimal philosophical anthropology and individual focus, however, Sen's philosophy alone is not sufficient to offer a fully human understanding of human rights and a sense of community in solidarity. Unlike Taylor's work, Sen's philosophy does not fully account for the dialogical nature of the self and solidarity as constitutive of the self. It is in the mutual relationship between human rights and solidarity in the human person that Catholic social teaching can offer useful insights for the larger field of human rights policy, practice, and activism. Through the study of the human person as a person in community, Catholic social teaching offers human rights and solidarity as necessary twin pillars for contemporary social ethics. In the following chapter, we will return to Catholic social teaching to deepen the understanding of solidarity. Not only are human rights and solidarity mutually dependent upon one another, but through the praxis of human rights we are called to cultivate and habituate the virtue of solidarity.

4

The Virtue of Solidarity and the Praxis of Human Rights

"As long as there is poverty in the world I can never be rich, even if I have a billion dollars. As long as diseases are rampant and millions of people in this world cannot expect to live more than twenty-eight or thirty years, I can never be totally healthy even if I just got a good checkup at Mayo Clinic. I can never be what I ought to be until you are what you ought to be. This is the way our world is made. No individual or nation can stand out boasting of being independent. We are interdependent."
Martin Luther King Jr.[1]

"The culture of selfishness and individualism that often prevails in our society is not what builds up and leads to a more habitable world: it is the culture of solidarity that does so, seeing others not as rivals or statistics, but brothers and sisters."
Pope Francis, Address to the Community of Varginha[2]

GROUNDING BOTH HUMAN RIGHTS AND SOLIDARITY IN THE HUMAN PERSON

Human dignity, as an ontological characteristic of the human person, includes relationality. Not only are human persons social by nature, but human dignity itself also includes relationality and participation. Through the previous chapters, examining in detail communal philosophical and theological

---

1. Martin Luther King Jr., *Measure of a Man* (Minneapolis: Fortress Press, 2001), 45–46.

2. Francis, "Address of Pope Francis," visit to the community of Varginha (Manguinhos), Brazil, July 25, 2013, http://www.vatican.va/holy_father/francesco/speeches/2013/july/documents/papa-francesco_20130725_gmg-comunita-varginha_en.html.

anthropologies, I have argued for human rights and solidarity as mutually necessary for any authentic human existence. Human dignity is characterized by equality, mutuality, and reciprocity. The goal of this section is to pull together the anthropological conclusions as the foundation for the assertion that human dignity mandates both human rights and solidarity. In particular, through the social matrix underpinning freedom, rationality, and the modern moral order, human dignity emerges as the value of equal human persons, but it cannot be grounded in a formal definition of freedom alone. Theologically, the *imago dei* understood as *imago trinitatis* offers a "unity across difference" and emphasizes the centrality of equality, mutuality, and reciprocity as the criteria by which to evaluate human relationships. Through the theological reflection on Trinity and covenant, Christian ethics offers a conception of human dignity that firmly binds together the individual and community, human rights, and solidarity. Finally, Amartya Sen's social analysis of development provides analytical support for the necessity of social and economic conditions for the realization of human rights. All of this provides, then, the ground for the relationship between the virtue of solidarity and the praxis of human rights within Catholic social teaching.

PHILOSOPHICAL ISSUES

As the human rights tradition developed, Immanuel Kant appears as a major reference point concerning freedom and human dignity. Both Pope John Paul II and Sen are influenced by Kant, and he represents a major figure in the narrative of modernity addressed by Charles Taylor. Dignity for Kant is grounded in the human capacity for self-legislation; the capacity for rational agency is the foundation of the kingdom of ends and human dignity.[3] As Taylor points out, this makes freedom purely formal or procedural, based on our ability to be a law unto ourselves and the universalizability thereof. John Paul II attempts to synthesize the categorical imperative with the gospel, finding the more contemporary language and universality appealing. In particular, the insight that all human persons are ends in themselves and can never be used as merely a means to an end resonates well with the arguments of Catholic social teaching. In this formal focus on the act, John Paul II uses Kant to highlight that we must recognize that other human persons, as agents, have their own ends—that human persons are capable of being both subject and object simultaneously. In his philosophical use of Kant, John Paul II adapts

---

3. Immanuel Kant, *Grounding for the Metaphysics of Morals*, trans. James W. Ellington (Indianapolis, IN: Hackett, 1993).

Kant in connection with his Thomistic personalism, phenomenology, and theological commitment to the Scripture. Still, for reasons highlighted earlier, Kant presents a number of philosophical problems for understanding the relationality of the person.

While the insight of the categorical imperative is crucial for the development of the modern moral order, Kant is insufficient for an adequate grounding of human rights, solidarity, and freedom. As Taylor explains, specifying certain capacities that are worthy of respect is insufficient without a correlative commitment to protect and promote such capacities.[4] Human capabilities are only developed within a social matrix, as chapter 2 demonstrates; therefore, a commitment to rational agency conceived entirely as involving individual consciousness is unsustainable. Moreover, within Kant's conception, moral demands must be subject to the universalizability principle.[5] While on the surface this appears to support universal human rights, the notion of autonomy is too individualistic to provide an adequate basis for the social relationships needed to sustain human dignity, human rights, and solidarity. Furthermore, it does not adequately admit the necessity of social structures, the support for substantial exercise of rational agency, and the development of a self-identity.

The specific problem with Sen's use of Kantian categories is revealed in the distinctions between perfect and imperfect obligations, as detailed in the previous chapter. Because of a purely individual and formal understanding of rationality and agency, the only obligations that include a clear ethical imperative to action are perfect obligations—my obligation not to violate the rational agency of another through a failure to recognize her status as a subject by treating her as a mere means or instrument. Perfect obligations, however, are negative in nature. They represent my perfect and binding obligation not to do X, where X is a violation of someone else's rights or dignity. Any obligation to prevent someone else from being murdered never translates to a perfect obligation. And imperfect obligations do not lead to obligations of action, only to obligations to rationally, reasonably, or seriously consider action. There are legitimate distinctions between one's moral obligations as the primary agent and one's moral obligations to intervene. However, Kant's individual focus on autonomy is insufficient to develop our moral obligations to intervene on behalf of others—that is, our moral obligations of solidarity. An interesting side effect of this particular Kantian influence is that while the individual person is never to be a mere means, the community appears to become just that.

4. Charles Taylor, "Atomism," in *Philosophical Papers*, vol. 2: *Philosophy and the Human Sciences* (Cambridge: Cambridge University Press, 1985), 194.
5. Kant, *Metaphysics of Morals*, 39.

Even as Sen admits the centrality of economic and social opportunities in developing substantive freedoms, he still does not offer a comprehensive or integrated understanding of the community as having integrity and value in itself. This represents a major difference between Sen's analysis of community in developing distinctively human capabilities and Taylor's communitarian philosophy of the person, which includes an obligation to belong.

For Taylor, responsibility with regard to freedom, agency, human rights, and the community cannot be purely negative. If one is committed to the concepts of freedom, human rights, and solidarity as worthy of respect and to be pursued, this must include a positive responsibility to foster and promote them. This duty does not rest merely in a duty to consider. Freedom and rationality are placed within the social matrix that makes them possible and allows them to develop, which includes an obligation to participate in and promote this social matrix for future generations. Therefore, the modern social imaginary has as its foundation the human person based in equality, mutual obligation, and modern instances or levels of community. And, as chapter 2 indicates, the modern social imaginary is both normative and descriptive. The socially embedded free person in Taylor's philosophy is characterized by a commitment to equality, mutuality, and reciprocity. Moreover, there is value and integrity to the community and relationality of the human person. From this positive understanding of obligation and moral responsibility, Taylor offers a rich philosophical exposition of human dignity from which human rights and solidarity are a natural development. The specific ways to positively promote dignity, human rights, and solidarity will be examined under the virtue of solidarity. Catholic social thought's foundation in Aquinas, in addition to Taylor's understanding of the social matrix and obligation to belong, provides a model of objective morality that is contextual. Objectivity is not dependent on strict universalizability. Furthermore, the universality of human rights and the one human family does not necessitate obligations as universal in a uniform way.

THEOLOGICAL ISSUES

Human persons are created in the image and likeness of God. Thus, the necessary starting point for any Christian reflection on human dignity is the *imago dei*. Not only are human persons endowed with freedom and rationality, but, based on Scripture and tradition, to be *imago dei* is to be *imago trinitatis*. An examination of *imago dei* through the contemporary Trinitarian theologies of Elizabeth Johnson, CSJ, and Catherine LaCugna places equality, mutuality, and reciprocity at the heart of any definition of the human person. Our understanding of the relationship among the three persons in one God is severely limited if we rest content with the inner life of the triune God as mystery. Despite this, however, Christian theology can affirm that the three persons in one Trinitarian God are characterized by equality, mutuality, and reciprocity. Thus, Elizabeth Johnson concludes, "God lives as a mystery of love. Human beings are created in the image of this God. Therefore, a life of integrity is impossible unless we also enter into the dynamic of love and communion with others."[6]

Human dignity then must be understood within the framework of the Trinity. While the Christian human rights tradition provides a long history of arguments grounding universal human rights in the equal dignity of each human person as a unique instance of the image of God, examining human dignity through the lens of the Trinity makes relationality an integral component of the *imago dei*. This is not simply a reassertion that the human is a rational *and* social animal. Instead, it is a claim about how that sociality should be understood and modeled. Moreover, John 17:20-22, in which Jesus prays "that they may be one as we are one," offers this Trinitarian model of equality, mutuality, and reciprocity as that toward which we should strive in our human relationships. If our common humanity is modeled and understood in light of the Trinity, then "I cannot be what I ought to be until you are what you ought to be."

This humanity, characterized by socially embedded freedom and rationality, as well as the dignity of being created in the image and likeness of God, requires both universal human rights and solidarity. Solidarity, then, is grounded in that same human dignity, that same philosophical and theological anthropology as grounds human rights. As a result, if human rights are inherent, inalienable, and universal, so too is the call to solidarity. Moreover, community is not ancillary to the human person but provides and conditions the social matrix required to develop rational agency and freedom. Given the strong sense of development of the person, I can be more or less free, more or less rational. Throughout our lives we are called to develop more fully human lives and communities. This is what the biblical covenants invite us into and instruct us about; it is the model of fidelity, mutuality, and reciprocity revealed within covenantal theology.

Understanding the *imago dei* as *imago trinitatis* requires that each individual human person is in the image and likeness of God and that *we*, as a community, are in the image and likeness of God. Through my choices, actions, and

6. Elizabeth A. Johnson, *Quest for the Living God* (New York: Continuum, 2007), 222.

responses I can become more or less fully human and more or less fully image God in the world. Through our choices, actions, and responses, we can become more or less fully human together and more or less fully image God in the world. We are less fully imaging God in the world while extreme poverty, oppression, exploitation, and violence continue. In short, through severe human rights violations we are less fully able to live as *imago dei*, and these violations represent a failure of solidarity.

"As long as there is poverty in the world I can never be rich, even if I have a billion dollars." Interdependence is not simply a matter of necessary survival but a function of what it means to be human. The dignity of *our* humanity is at stake. This affects every individual human person, not only the victims. This is what it means to be a human person: to be free and responsible, to be rational and relational, and that relationality includes every other human person. Participation is participation in the humanity of the other so that when we sacrifice them, or allow them to be sacrificed, we are sacrificing ourselves. Our common humanity is the risk, benefit, and demand of human dignity; it requires human rights and solidarity.

SOCIAL ANALYTIC ENGAGEMENT

Despite the critiques and limitations of Sen's thought already presented, *Development as Freedom* provides considerable analytic and quantitative support for the necessary role of the community in realizing human rights. Through Sen's work on human rights and development, it is clear that there can be no future without development and no development without substantive freedoms. Capabilities and substantive freedoms—instead of income, gross national product, or a purely legal civil-political liberty—recognize the centrality of social structures and economic conditions for the sustainability and reliability of human rights. Broadening the conception of freedom, Sen offers rigorous social analysis that demands an integrated approach to human rights and can be used to provide support for the integral development in Catholic social teaching's moral vision. Moreover, he provides clear arguments for the importance of a theory of human rights and continued intellectual scrutiny of all human rights theory. He explains:

> Human rights activists are often quite impatient with such critiques. The invoking of human rights tends to come mostly from those who are concerned with changing the world rather than interpreting it. . . . However, the conceptual doubts must also be satisfactorily addressed, if the idea of human rights is to command reasoned loyalty

and to establish a secure intellectual standing. It is critically important
to see the relationship between the force and appeal of human rights,
on the one hand, and their reasoned justification and scrutinized use,
on the other.[7]

Thus, Sen's writings and the work of the United Nations Development
Programme offer quantitative and analytical analysis as dialogue partners and
clear intellectual support for a reasoned and well-articulated theory of human
rights.

RETURNING TO CATHOLIC SOCIAL TEACHING: CLARIFYING THE VIRTUE OF SOLIDARITY AND ITS RELATIONSHIP TO HUMAN RIGHTS

Human rights and solidarity emerge as mutually dependent and necessary
in order to constitute an authentically human person or community. This
is demonstrated by the presence of both in recent Catholic social teaching's
reflections on emerging global ethical concerns. While the encyclicals do not
explicitly explain the connection between human rights and solidarity, the
foundational philosophical and theological anthropology explains why human
rights and solidarity require each other. From Pope John XXIII to Pope
Benedict XVI, human rights are used with precision and a specification of both
the rights and the moral obligations attached to individuals, communities, and
nations. On contrast, solidarity remains surrounded by a degree of ambiguity.
Beginning with the growing awareness of interdependence and the moral
importance of integral development in the 1970s, the concept of solidarity as
a moral category was somewhat elusive as it was characterized as a feeling, an
attitude, a duty, and finally a virtue. In particular, if solidarity is a virtue, how
does one habituate this virtue? What are the practices by which one acquires
the virtue of solidarity? For Catholic social teaching, clarifying solidarity based
on the philosophical and theological anthropology I have described involves
examining how solidarity is at once an attitude, a duty, and a virtue. The
purpose of this section is to detail the three levels of solidarity as found in
Catholic social teaching. This examination is illuminated by the philosophical
anthropology of Taylor and the theology of the person as *imago trinitatis*,
and this section concludes with an explication of the virtue of solidarity as
habituated through the practices of human rights.

7. Amartya Sen, "Elements of a Theory of Human Rights," *Philosophy & Public Affairs* 32, no. 4
(Autumn 2004): 317.

First, solidarity is an attitude; this is the descriptive element of solidarity. Thus, according to Pope Paul VI, "there can be no progress toward complete development of man without the development of all humanity in the spirit of solidarity" (PP 43). Just as John Paul II recognizes the positive growing awareness among peoples of their dignity and human rights, so there is an awareness or attitude of interdependence: "the conviction is growing of a *radical interdependence* and consequently of the need for a solidarity which will take interdependence and transfer it to the moral plane" (SRS 26). This growing inclination begins with a natural awareness that human persons are interdependent and is a direct consequence of the approach to human dignity in the previous section. The attitude of solidarity begins with the descriptive recognition of radical interdependence and presents this interdependence as a necessary variable for ethical reflection and decision making.

As the epigraph of Martin Luther King Jr. states quite simply, *we are interdependent*. For Taylor, this is the recognition of the "dialogical nature of the person." The "self," as such, can only be developed and constructed within a social matrix. Theologically, this begins with the recognition that human society is present within the very creation account (Gen. 1:26-27) and the awareness that it is not good for the human person to be alone: "For his innermost nature man is a social being, and unless he relates himself to others, he can neither live nor develop his potential" (GS 12). Solidarity as an attitude is a descriptive awareness of this reality. Sen's social analysis provides empirical evidence for both the reality of interdependence and the growing awareness or attitude of solidarity. Throughout *Development as Freedom*, the insistence on social opportunities, which he includes in his definition of *substantive freedom* as human rights, is a recognition of the interdependence that is the reality of human existence. Thus, as the 1971 Synod of Bishops states: "The crisis of universal solidarity . . . economic injustice and lack of social participation keep man from attaining his basic human and civil rights" (JM 1.9).[8] This, then, is the first level of solidarity espoused by Catholic social teaching, which is grounded in a relational anthropology (both philosophical and theological) prioritizing both human rights and community. Already within Sen's focus on *substantive freedom*, the recognition of interdependence and an attitude of solidarity are necessary for the enhancement of human rights. At this level solidarity remains a descriptive category; however, this first descriptive level prompts the normative ethical levels of duty and virtue.

---

8. Synod of Bishops, *Justitia in Mundo*, in *Catholic Social Thought: The Documentary Heritage*, ed. David J. O'Brien and Thomas A Shannon (Maryknoll, NY: Orbis, 1992), 289.

Building on the first descriptive level, the second level of solidarity is *duty*. Paul VI explains, "It is not just certain individuals, but all men who are called to this fullness of development. . . . We have inherited from past generations and we have benefited from the work of our contemporaries: for this reason, we have obligations toward all . . . the reality of human solidarity, which as a benefit for us also imposes a duty" (PP 17). As a normative ethical category, the duty of solidarity applies both to individuals and communities (small and large). Within the duty of solidarity is the requirement of mutuality, reciprocity, and equal regard in human rights. Human rights have implicit within them the duty to respect the rights of others. This duty of mutuality includes the obligation of the state to recognize the rights of all persons. In his explication of human rights in *Pacem in Terris*, John XXIII examines three levels of duties within human rights, the first two of which fall into this level of solidarity. They are the duty of mutuality already mentioned, and the correlative duty latent within each human right (such as the duty to live life fully and becomingly as a correlative to the right to life). On the individual level this correlative duty appears to be a matter of human rights and not solidarity; however, one is not able to fulfill the correlative individual duties of human rights except in relation to others. I cannot live life becomingly in isolation. Furthermore, once one admits there are rights of communities in addition to rights of individuals, then the correlative duty of communities or nations becomes not only a matter of human rights but also of solidarity.

This second aspect of the duty of solidarity is made explicit in Taylor's "The Politics of Recognition," in which he details the imperative of the political processes of mutual respect and participation to include not only individuals but also the distinctiveness of communities. For Taylor, as for Catholic social teaching, the duty of solidarity includes those duties associated with protecting the human rights of communities as well as individuals. The awareness or attitude of solidarity involves the acknowledgment that human persons were created in and for community. This is also true in the biblical covenants where human persons are related to God through communities of interdependence. The duty of solidarity, however, points theologically to the equal dignity of each human person as created in the image and likeness of God (*imago dei*). As such, each individual is obliged to recognize that each other person is *imago dei*, that equality, mutuality, and reciprocity place a claim upon the human person.

Development provides an important example of how duty, as the second level of solidarity, functions. Sen's social analysis in relation to the duty of solidarity and human rights is both insightful and limited. Sen extends his conception of human rights to include all *substantive freedoms*, highlighting the importance of development for human rights and for the development of the person (capabilities). Thus, Sen specifically includes social and economic opportunities among rights. There is a duty not to directly violate the human rights of another person. The duty is that of the perfect obligation, which is the duty of an individual agent (or community of agents) to not directly violate the rights of others. Perfect obligations are limited to one's own role as primary agent. This only includes my duty not to murder, torture, economically exploit, or persecute a particular individual or group directly. It does not extend to a duty to intercede to stop someone else from committing any of these acts against another person or group; one only has an obligation to seriously or reasonably consider doing so, which is the imperfect obligation. What Sen does not provide is a duty to act to protect or promote respect for human rights by others or on their behalf. This is the imperfect obligation; there is no duty of intervention on behalf of human rights. The limitations of the imperfect obligation are more central, however, to the third and final level of solidarity.

The culmination of solidarity is the virtue of solidarity.[9] The third level directly builds on the attitude and duty levels, continuing to incorporate both the awareness of interdependence and the obligations to respect human rights and to develop solidarity within the cultivation, practice, and acquisition of the virtue. The substantive meaning of solidarity, as a virtue, includes not only political or social conditions but also commitment to personal flourishing and the participation in the universal common good. According to *Sollicitudo Rei Socialis*, the virtue of solidarity "is not a feeling of vague compassion or shallow distress at the misfortunes of so many people, both near and far. On the contrary, it is a *firm and persevering determination* to commit oneself to the *common good*; that is to say to the good of all and of each individual because we are really *all* responsible *for all*" (SRS 38). The dignity of the individual and the human community are preconditions here, and yet, as Benedict XVI notes in *Caritas in Veritate*, we must accept the call of solidarity and responsibility for and to each other (CV 11). Moreover, this duty of individuals is simultaneously an obligation of communities and nations (PP 48). Not only is solidarity a virtue, it is a social virtue. Catholic social teaching is clear that this is so, but what does it mean to state that solidarity is a social virtue? How do I know that I have the virtue of solidarity? What exactly is required by this virtue? To whom does it apply? By what practices is it acquired? And what, if any, are corresponding

---

9. An analogous correlative to this multifaceted understanding of solidarity as principle, duty, and virtue is the Catholic social ethics approach to justice, which also has principles and duties, and culminates in the virtue of justice.

vices? The virtue of solidarity is in fact both an individual virtue and a social virtue. By offering an examination of *the anatomy of this social virtue*, one begins to see the scope and boundaries of solidarity, corresponding sets of vices for this virtue, and how communities can cultivate this virtue through practicing respect for human rights.

SOLIDARITY AS A VIRTUE

In asserting that solidarity is virtue, John Paul II placed solidarity within a long list of moral virtues in the tradition of virtue ethics, including prudence, justice, and fortitude, among others. [10][11] For Aristotle, the possibility of virtue began within the quality and capacity (or capabilities) of human nature and the ability to turn this natural capacity to human action. Moral virtue "is formed by habit," and through this habituation process it becomes second nature, or a firm character.[12] Explaining the criteria for a person to engage in virtuous action, Aristotle states: "first of all, he must know what he is doing; secondly, he must choose to act the way he does, and he must choose it for its own sake and in the third place, the act must spring from a firm and unchanging character."[13] In order for actions and habits to lead to moral virtue, the act in question must conform to practical reason and must be done at the right time and place and for the right reasons.[14] This emphasis on intentional acceptance of responsibility pervades Catholic social teaching's

10. An earlier version of this section appears as "Anatomy of a Social Virtue: Solidarity and Corresponding Vices" *Political Theology* 15. No1 (2014) a special issue on the theme of solidarity.

11. This chapter will briefly refer to the basic accounts of virtue in Aristotle's *Nichomachean Ethics* and St. Thomas Aquinas's *Summa Theologiae*. In addition to being classic texts on virtue, St. Thomas Aquinas (himself strongly influenced by Aristotle) is the intellectual foundation for Catholic social teaching more generally. Therefore, while there is a substantial literature on virtue ethics and contemporary theories of virtue, the definitions provided here will be limited to these classic accounts.

12. Aristotle, *Nichomachean Ethics*, trans. Martin Ostwald (Upper Saddle River, NJ: Prentice Hall, 1999), book 2, 33.

13. Aristotle, *Nichomachean Ethics*, 39.

14. Bonnie Kent explains, "The English word [habit] tends to mislead insofar as habit can signify for English speakers any routine performance, however trivial or mechanical. . . . A *hexis* or *habitus*, in contrast, is a durable characteristic of the agent inclining to certain kinds of actions and emotional reactions, not the actions and reactions themselves. Acquired over time, habits grow to be 'second nature' for the individual." Bonnie Kent, "Habits and Virtues (Ia IIae, qq. 49–70)," in *The Ethics of Aquinas*, ed. Stephen J. Pope (Washington, DC: Georgetown University Press, 2002), 116. It is important to note, Kent explains, that acquiring virtuous habits is a distinctively human capacity: "Thomas believes that even the best-trained animals always act from instinct. . . . In his view, human beings are blamed for tantrums, fits of gluttony, and other such actions because we never act from passion without the consent of our wills. Animals cannot fairly be blamed for similar behavior."

attention to solidarity. It is particularly emphasized by Benedict XVI, who explains that "integral human development presupposes the responsible freedom of the individual and of peoples" (CV 17). Structures and institutions are crucial; however, solidarity cannot be present without the positive freedom of people to pursue the common good. Therefore, these habits must be formed through rational and freely chosen actions; unconscious habitual actions (such as a nervous tic) or coerced actions cannot lead to virtue.

Developing moral virtue is a process.[15] Through habituation, a virtue is acquired as a disposition to judge, act, will, and feel well or rightly in accordance with practical reason. The focal point of this process is the combination of human agency and human dignity. What does this look like in solidarity? As a virtue, which can be acquired by both individuals and communities, solidarity is built on a holistic and participatory understanding of human agency.

The human agency presupposed in this account of solidarity begins with human persons as socially embedded and as *self-interpreting animals*, to use the language of Taylor. He explains that this distinguishes us from even the most intelligent and social animals: "The dolphin, for all its intelligence and sociality, never has to be asked what it means to be a dolphin. For human agents, however, the question of what it means to be a human being is always an open question, always open to interpretation."[16] Moreover, this self-interpretation or strong evaluation requires asking oneself crucial questions: What kind of person do I wish to be? What kind of community do we wish to become? Moral virtues within Catholic social teaching are framed by the call to realize more fully human lives within a more fully human community. In the very concept of social virtue, we are extending these moral questions of identity and becoming to communities of persons.

To properly examine solidarity as a social virtue, a few key elements of virtues must first be identified. As illustrated by the classic virtue theories of Aquinas and Aristotle, as well as the theories proffered by contemporary virtue ethics, all virtues must have clear objects and ends. For solidarity, the formal object is our common humanity. The end of solidarity is participation in the universal common good. To be more specific, it is the participation by all

---

15. St. Thomas Aquinas, *Summa Theologiae*, trans. Fathers of the English Dominican Province (Allen, TX: Christian Classics, 1991), IaIIae.49.4.corp; all Aquinas references are from this edition. Note that this is also why for Aquinas all human action is either morally good or morally bad, as alluded to in the previous chapter.

16. Terry Pinkard, "Taylor and History of Philosophy," in *Charles Taylor*, ed. Ruth Abbey (Cambridge: Cambridge University Press, 2004), 191.

in the universal common good.[17] Participation is emphasized here along with the common good because the virtue of solidarity cannot be achieved without active, unified participation. The equality of persons mandates this. As such, the end of the virtue of solidarity is connected to Martin Luther King Jr.'s profound conclusion that "I cannot be what I ought to be until you are what you ought to be." What precisely does that mean?

Populorum Progressio provides three helpful examples of practices or requirements of solidarity: the aid rich countries offer to developing ones, the duty of social justice in the area of trade relations, and a duty of "universal charity" (PP 44). These are three instances of concrete practices by which rich societies may cultivate a social virtue of solidarity. However, on face value, these practices alone on the part of rich countries do not necessarily represent practices of solidarity for two essential reasons. First, the virtue of solidarity, rooted in the human person, cannot be realized without recognition of equal human dignity. Without equality and recognition of universal human rights, acts or habits of solidarity are impossible. Second, rich nations giving aid to developing nations in the form of simple almsgiving or charity, and without engagement or input from the receiving nation, does not afford the requisite agency for the presence of solidarity. Development aid can manifest solidarity if it involves active participation, cognizance of human rights, and subsidiarity. Abiding these preconditions, aid attends to the many levels of community and institutions in society, and the act is properly directed to the end of solidarity.[18]

The virtue of solidarity requires the participation of both the "agent" and those with whom the "agent" seeks to be in solidarity. While other virtues, especially individual ones such as temperance, courage, or self-care, may focus on the habits and agency of the individual, social virtue must contemplate agency in terms of participation. Within the example of aid given by rich countries to developing ones, this requires not only the input of the government of the developing country, but also a meaningful connection to the processes and movements of development among the people in said

17. Given that solidarity is treated as the fundamental social virtue, according to the *Compendium on the Social Doctrine of the Church*, it is worth noting that this is the proximate end insofar as the ultimate end of solidarity would be the kingdom of God. See Catholic Church, Pontificium Consilium de Iustitia et Pace, *Compendium of the Social Doctrine of the Church* (Vatican City: Veritas, 2005), http://www.vatican.va/roman_curia/pontifical_councils/justpeace/documents/ rc_pc_justpeace_doc_20060526_compendio-dott-soc_en.html.

18. Cf. CV, 58: "Economic aid, in order to be true to its purpose, must not pursue secondary objectives. It must be distributed with the involvement not only of the governments of receiving countries, but also the local economic agents and the bearers of culture within civil society, including local Churches."

country. In order to qualify as the virtue of solidarity, practices and participation cannot be one-sided and must include the agency of all persons and moral agents within the particular context. The equality, mutuality, and reciprocity of human dignity must be present. Without this, those with whom one group wishes to be *in solidarity* are not acknowledged and respected as full members of the one human community or family. Thus, as the end of solidarity indicates, the virtue of solidarity involves a *firm and persevering determination* to both individual dignity and the integrity of communities. Neither the individual nor the common good can be eliminated or sacrificed in solidarity as directed toward its proper end. Before turning to the process by which the community acquires solidarity as a social virtue, it is helpful to consider solidarity in contrast to related vices in which either the individual or community is sacrificed.

A VIRTUE BETWEEN VICES

Virtue begins with habits and natural capacities. Given that natural capacities, feelings, emotions, and attitudes can be experienced disproportionately in extremes, virtue is directed at the mean. Aristotle explains, "We can experience fear, confidence, desire, anger, pity, and generally any kind of pleasure and pain either too much or too little, and in either case not properly. But, to experience all this at the right time, toward the right objects, toward the right people, for the right reason and in the right manner—that is the median and best course, the course that is a mark of virtue."[19] A virtue is not simply the *middle* but navigates between excess and deficiency through the use of practical reason or prudence directed to the common good. This is contrasted with vices, which by definition are not properly ordered.[20]

Aristotle's virtue of courage comes immediately to mind. The natural feeling or capacity is one's response in the face of fear. Courage is the virtue, a response to fear grounded in practical reason and directed toward the common good. A lack of courage, or the vice of deficiency, is cowardice and the failure of fortitude in the face of danger. Concurrently, the vice of excess, or rashness, evokes a lack of rational fear in the face of danger. The virtue of courage is found in the mean, acting without cowardice or excess, and properly ordered by practical reason toward the common good.

---

19. Aristotle, *Nichomachean Ethics*, 43. In Christian ethics, particularly the virtue theory of St. Thomas Aquinas, charity is the one virtue that is not a mean because it does not have a vice of excess.

20. This occurs through the virtue of prudence. For a fuller examination of Prudence see St. Thomas Aquinas, *Summa Theologiae*, IIa IIae, q. 47–56; and James F. Keenan, SJ, "The Virtue of Prudence (IIa IIae, q. 47–56)," in Pope, *Ethics of Aquinas*, 259–71.

Solidarity, like courage, is the mean—a virtue between vices. However, solidarity is situated between types of vices, which can be applied to individual persons, communities, and entire societies. Moreover, given the dialogical complexities of solidarity, which are grounded in both the end of the virtue and the view of the human person, its corresponding vices may function on many levels of individuals and communities. These vices all involve a causal nexus between individual adoption of a vicious worldview to the group establishment of larger and larger communities and structures founded upon this insufficient view of the human person.

Vice, and not merely sin, is the appropriate moral category, as moral theologian Daniel Daly notes, because "injustice is not an action per se, but instead, is a vice which produces discrete moral acts which are often sinful. This is not merely semantics, but a conceptual development."[21] This understanding of social vice builds upon recent scholarship on *structures of vice*, or "the social structures that in some way consistently function to prevent the human good, the common good, and human happiness, and, the socially rooted moral habits willingly internalized by moral agents that consistently prescribe sinful human acts, and produce human unhappiness."[22] These structures of vice, which are manifest in unjust institutions and social structures, work to create social vice insofar as these sinful habits are habituated not only by individuals but communities of persons.

The primary vice of deficiency is *excessive individualism*, which presumes that human persons are fundamentally isolated, atomized individuals or blank slates.[23] Under these sets of vices, human persons are individuals by nature, and social or interdependent by choice. One popular example of this is the illusion of *Robinson Crusoe* and the subtraction view of modernity.[24] From this perspective, modernity is primarily about stripping away and shrugging off confining social structures; freedom is achieved by removing external constraints. While egoism is perhaps the clearest example of this vice of

21. Daniel J. Daly, "Structures of Virtue and Vice," *New Blackfriars* 92 (2011): 356.

22. Ibid, 355.

23. For extensive definition of excessive individualism versus legitimate self-interest see Angus Sibley, *The "Poisoned Spring" of Economic Libertarianism: Menger, Mises, Hayek, Rothbard; a Critique from Catholic Social Teaching of the "Austrian School" of Economics* (Washington, DC: Pax Romana, 2011).

24. The subtraction view of modernity is treated in depth in the philosophy of Charles Taylor, who explains it as an attempt to reclaim the Enlightenment in which one, as a socially embedded individual, "imagin[es] oneself as belonging to an even wider and more impersonal entities: the state, the movement, the community of human kind." *Modern Social Imaginaries* (Durham, NC: Duke University Press, 2004), 160).

deficiency, any social organization in which social groups or communities are purely functional or instrumental represents it.

The starting point for the vice is the conception of the human person. Despite the fact that there may be some pragmatic agreements on some ethical practices or conclusions, the worldview is fundamentally incompatible. As Angus Sibley notes, "excessive individualist morality insists that each person must live by his own efforts and avoid dependence on others. It takes a dim view of notions of solidarity and interdependence."[25] In *Caritas in Veritate*, Benedict XVI cautions against this excessive individualism, or "*social privatism*" that is latent in calls for subsidiarity without proper attention to solidarity (CV 38). Egoism and libertarianism undermine the fundamental teachings of Judeo-Christian morality concerning the poor, the community, and the common good. Libertarianism is one example of such a vice that is at once a philosophical claim and form of political organization. The social vice of excessive individualism also includes *homo economicus*, or the view of man primarily as self-interested, defining rationality itself as individual self-interest.[26] Another economic instance of individualism is a community built upon pure laissez-faire economics.[27] Whether rooted in philosophy, politics, or economics, all of the social structures built on this isolated view of the person foster the social vice of individualism and a false sense of the human condition.

In all of these cases, an atomized vision of the person as individual, often even further atomized to a particular aspect of the individual, is taken as the flawed foundation of all further social relationships. Part of what raises this to the level of social vice is that, by operating at all levels of society, these instantiations of excessive individualism create a false consciousness that is adopted like a second nature. Various instances of the social vice of individualism combine and collide in the vision of philosopher and novelist Ayn Rand. The central underlying premise of Rand's philosophy is her understanding of rational self-interest. Human persons are fundamentally isolated individuals in which rationality is tied to selfishness. Rand explains: "The rational interests of men do not clash—that there is no conflict of interests of men who do not desire what is unearned, who do not make sacrifices nor

25. Sibley, *Poisoned Spring of Economic Libertariansim*, 38.

26. For example, the Austrian School of Economics, most notably, Friedrich von Hayek. For more information see two of his books: *Individualism and Economic Order* (Chicago: University of Chicago Press, 1948); and *The Constitution of Liberty* (London: Routledge, 1960).

27. Most notably, Milton Friedman, *Capitalism and Freedom*, Fortieth Anniversary Edition (Chicago: University of Chicago Press, 2002); and Milton Friedman and Rose Friedman, *Free to Choose: A Personal Statement* (New York: Mariner Books, 1990)

accept them, who deal with one another as traders, giving value for value."[28] This "virtue of selfishness" as underlying rationality coincides with Rand's commitment to pure, unregulated capitalism and a complete "separation of state and economics." Excessive individualism, then, is built upon a false understanding of the human person and, in the case of Rand's libertarianism, seeks to metastasize the personal vice of selfishness into the very foundation not only of social relationships but of rationality itself.

This false consciousness and vicious *second nature* reached a recent public culmination in Alan Greenspan's testimony to the United States Congress in the wake of the 2008 financial crisis. Greenspan admits that he did not foresee the crisis because it was wholly incompatible with his overarching worldview.[29] In his October 23, 2008 statement before Congress, Greenspan admitted, "Those of us who looked to self-interest of lending institutions to protect shareholder equity are in a state of shocked disbelief."[30] House Government and Oversight Committee Chairman Henry Waxman then confronted Greenspan with his own statement that "I [Greenspan] do have an ideology. My judgment is that free, competitive markets are by far the unrivaled way to organize economies. We've tried regulation. None meaningfully worked."[31] Waxman sought to corner Greenspan into an admission that his worldview showed flaws in light of the financial crisis. Greenspan responded by pointing out that an ideology "is a conceptual framework with the way people deal with reality. Everyone has one . . . and what I'm saying to you is yes, I found a flaw." He went on to express his distress in finding "a flaw in the model that I perceived as the critical functioning structure that defines how the world works."

The assumption that rational self-interest will lead to proper industrial self-regulation relates to the vision of the human person in excessive individualism. Greenspan's testimony before Congress is one concrete example demonstrating the role of identity (individual and communal) in questions of social virtue and vice. The impact of this still reverberates in the global financial structure. The depth and embeddedness of this social vice in the financial sector is still being

28. Quote from "The Objectivist Ethics," delivered at the University of Wisconsin Symposium, "Ethics in Our Time," in Madison, Wisconsin, on February 9, 1961, and later published in *The Virtue of Selfishness* (1961), http://www.aynrand.org/site/ PageServer?pagename=ari_ayn_rand_the_objectivist_ethics.

29. Cf. PBS, "The Warning," *Frontline*, 2009, http://www.pbs.org/wgbh/pages/frontline/warning/ view/

30. All quotes from Greenspan can be found in his 2008 testimony before Congress. See http://video.cnbc.com/gallery/?video=901309320 (transcript: http://www.washingtontimes.com/blog/ potus-notes/2008/oct/24/he-found-flaw/)

31. Ibid.

revealed (the Libor scandal is another of many examples). At the other extreme is found the vice of excess, or any form of collectivism in which persons are subsumed or subverted by the whole. This vice can take many forms, including communism, which treats individuals purely as parts in the whole (mechanism), and strict utilitarianism, in which the good of the individual can be overlooked on the basis of the greatest happiness of the many.[32] These represent both vices of excess within political philosophy, despite their differences. Economic manifestations of the vice of collectivism can be found within the ideology of corporate personhood, in which actual human persons are subsumed and subverted within the corporation that then becomes *the person*.

In the capitalist mechanism, individual workers, local communities, and others lose their unique dignity and are interchangeable based on use.[33] By extension, within the capitalist structure, corporate practices that directly violate concepts of human dignity, labor justice, and environmental regulations are accepted insofar as the fines associated with "getting caught" are preferable to actual changes in overarching business practices required to deal in a just manner with workers, communities, and the environment.[34] In 2013, the debate about the minimum wage and wage theft led to strikes by low-wage workers at McDonald's and elsewhere.[35] Reporting on the story, Henry Blodget at BusinessInsider.com focused on one businessman's tweet. The tweet is the capitalistic mechanism summed up in 140 characters: "They are costs. Full Stop. They don't have a stake, they hold nothing. They trade their labor for money."[36] In his column, Blodget responded, "Employees are human beings. They are people who devote their lives to creating value for customers, shareholders, and colleagues. . . . American business culture has become so

32. Standard representations of collectivism are Karl Marx (communism) and Jeremy Bentham and John Stuart Mill (utilitarianism).

33. The term *capitalist mechanism* is used here to draw attention to the mechanism operative in contemporary corporate capitalism that is akin to the mechanism of socialism attacked in Catholic social teaching from 1891 onward.

34. The practice by Walmart of forcing unpaid overtime while simultaneously actively blocking all attempts by workers to organize is an example of this. "Wage theft" within a system of coercion and vulnerability was exposed through a series of court cases and class actions in the early 2000s (despite nominal corporate policy to the contrary). Cf. Miguel De La Torre, *Doing Christian Ethics from the Margins* (Maryknoll, NY: Orbis, 2004), 213–19.

35. "Fast Foot Strike Continues Nationwide," *Democracy Now*, August 1, 2013, http://www.democracynow.org/2013/8/1/headlines/fast_food_retail_strike_continues_nationwide.

36. Tweet: Daryl Tremblay (@DarylT), July 30, 2013, quoted in Henry Blodget, "This One Tweet Reveals What's Wrong with American Business Culture and the Economy," *Business Insider*, August 1, 2013, http://www.businessinsider.com/business-and-the-economy-2013-7.

obsessed with maximizing short-term profits that employees aren't regarded as people who are members of a team."[37] As Pope John Paul II explains, "A society is alienated if its forms of social organization, production and consumption make it more difficult to offer this gift of self and to establish this solidarity between people" (CA 41). Moreover, the alienation of the capitalistic mechanism continues when work "is organized so as to ensure maximum returns and profits with no concern whether the worker, through his own labour, grows or diminishes as a person, either through increased sharing in a genuinely supportive community or through increased isolation in a maze of relationships marked by destructive competitiveness and estrangement, in which he is considered only a means and not an end" (CA 41). Both corporate personhood and the capitalist mechanism fail to respect the dignity of the person and other communities within the culture and structures of institutional practices. In *Centesimus Annus*, John Paul II cautioned, "When man does not recognize in himself and in others the value and grandeur of the human person, he deprives himself of the possible benefit from humanity and of entering into the relationships of solidarity and communion with others for which God created him" (CA 41).

Table 1. Solidarity and **Corresponding Vices**

	Social Vice of Deficiency: Individualism	**Social Virtue:** Solidarity	**Social Vice of Excess:**Collectivism
Basic definition of groups:	Structures built upon a Robinson-Crusoe vision of the human personIntegrity and dignity of community is violated or diminished	"Solidarity must be seen above all in its value and as a moral virtue that determines the order of institutions. On this basis of this principle the 'structures of sin' . . . must be purified and	Structures in which the individual is subsumed by the whole; individual human dignity violated or diminished

37. Ibid.

		transformed into *structures of solidarity* through the creation or appropriate modification of laws, market regulations, and juridical systems." (Compendium 193)	
Political philosophy	LibertarianismSocial privatism	S O L I D A R I T Y	Communism/ socialism
Philosophy	Egoism		Act/Strict utilitarianism
Economic	Laissez–faire capitalism*Homo economicus*		Capitalistic mechanism Corporate personhood
International Affairs	Nationalistic isolationism		Neocolonialism

CULTIVATING THE SOCIAL VIRTUE OF SOLIDARITY

Modern Catholic social teaching, from its inception with *Rerum Novarum* (*On the Condition of Labor*) during the Industrial Revolution in 1891, has attempted to articulate this social virtue and the commitment to both individual human dignity and the common good in contrast to these many vices of individualism and collectivism. Thus, the paradigm of the chart above is familiar to students of the Catholic social encyclicals. While most organizations or societies tend toward one end or the other of a graduated spectrum, the truly virtuous society would conceptually be one of solidarity, in which the integrity, uniqueness, and equality of individuals, as well as the integrity of the community and the universal common good, are promoted and protected. Solidarity, then, is a virtue of both persons and communities. This brings us back to the question of how a community or social group can cultivate and habituate the virtue of solidarity. Doing so requires the cultivation of practices that habituate solidarity as well as *structures of virtue*.[38]

As the *Compendium on the Social Doctrine of the Church* summarizes, "On the basis of this principle the 'structures of sin' that dominate relationships between individuals and peoples must be overcome. They must be purified and transformed into *structures of solidarity* through the creation or appropriate modification of laws, market regulations, and juridical systems."[39] The concepts of structures of sin and social vice are necessarily connected. Where structures of sin (or structures of vice, as an emerging alternative language) focus on the necessary and important role of institutions and structures, the understanding of social virtue and social vice presented here attempts to push beyond that question to the moral community's identity formed by these structures. Where Daly notes, "two loci of moral analysis: the social structures themselves; and the moral agents that form the social structures and are formed by participation in social structures," I propose a third locus—that of the community.[40] One concrete way a community can cultivate the social virtue of solidarity is through practicing respect for human rights, more specifically through the positive duties of active participation and the promotion of human rights. Once again, the specific requirements for solidarity are best illustrated through counterexamples of duties and virtues that are similar but not identical to solidarity—namely, negative duties with regard to human rights and the virtue of justice.

As it is most commonly understood, practicing human rights requires not directly or actively violating the human rights of others. Perhaps the clearest examples are habitually not engaging in torture and not suppressing another's freedom of religion. This is a negative duty that both persons and communities can fulfill. However, while this negative duty is required by both justice and the very conception of human rights, it does not rise to the virtue of solidarity, as it is not adequately directed toward the end of solidarity—participation in the universal common good of all.

Beyond this negative injunction, how do we practice respect for human rights? How do we fulfill the obligation to belong and the requirements of

38. Daly, "Structures of Virtue and Vice," 355.

39. Catholic Church, *Compendium of the Social Doctrine*, 193.

40. Daly, "Structures of Virtue and Vice," 356.

participation? According to Catholic social teaching, our obligation with regard to human rights also includes a positive requirement to promote these rights. Promoting human rights by focusing on substantive freedoms involves practicing acts that support and create economic and social opportunities such as education and access to health care. Within the context of the social virtue of solidarity, this incorporates the related principle of subsidiarity, in which decisions should be made at the closest level possible or the highest level necessary, recognizing the need of all levels of society (family, local, regional, national, global). The virtue of solidarity involves an obligation to participate at all levels of human community. Through the practices of promoting human rights, we can see examples of concrete ways social groups can manifest and habituate the social virtue of solidarity.

Imagine a situation where human rights are subverted, ignored, or violated. The specific obligations for moral action, in a particular instance, depend upon the circumstances and capabilities of those involved. Individuals and communities must ask how they can help. What is sought by those affected? What is the violation to human dignity occurring? What is the risk of action or inaction? Answers to these questions are required to determine the prudent action. This moral obligation to practice human rights can be realized through small actions, such as a personal boycott of a company that exploits workers or by writing letters to public officials, or larger, systematic, and coordinated actions by groups, communities, states, and the international community, such as the current Save Darfur movement.[41] However, this further step of participation and engagement with those whose rights are being violated must be present. Is the letter, boycott, or activism campaign informed by the perspective of those being oppressed? Is my own identity and dignity on the table? If I am not willing to be equally present in the encounter, then it cannot cultivate solidarity. This moral recognition of interdependence not only in terms of function but in terms of dignity and identity connects to Martin Luther King Jr.'s vision of an unified humanity.

As a social virtue, solidarity can manifest itself as opposition among small groups. Unified opposition in the face of injustice and human rights violations—in which a group of people are bonded in their common humanity, are demanding their dignity be acknowledged, and are seeking to be granted participation in the social order (political, economic, or civil)—is a clear example of the social virtue. Groups united by the virtue of solidarity are not merely unified in a cause or against an oppressor; instead, they are unified in the positive, active assertion of their own common humanity. Further, if the virtue

41. Save Darfur, a project of United to End Genocide, www.savedarfur.org.

of solidarity is to be cultivated, there must be participation and equality of human persons. While the actions may differ among different agents or circumstances, the virtue of solidarity through the practices of human rights strives for an integrated community in which we progressively move toward equality, mutuality, and reciprocity in our very interdependence itself. Reflecting on the common good, David Hollenbach says, "It is the good that comes into existence in a community of solidarity among active, equal agents. The common good, understood this way, is not extrinsic to the relationships that prevail among the members and sub-communities of a society. When these relationships form reciprocal ties among equals, the solidarity achieved itself a good that cannot otherwise exist."[42] As such, solidarity can exist as both an individual and a communal virtue—blossoming in each level of society and culminating in our common humanity.

In this way, the virtue of solidarity is linked to justice. The end of justice is to give that which is due and right to another.[43] Unlike justice, however, solidarity, through participation, connects oneself and the other in a way that justice alone does not. It is possible to advocate for human rights and practice respect for human rights in such a way as to meet the demands of justice without fulfilling the demands of solidarity. If the focus is entirely on the other, their rights, and helping them without investment of myself, my humanity, and my dignity, then the action fulfills justice, insofar as it is about rectifying an injustice and giving that which is due to another—their human rights. However, it does not fulfill solidarity. The virtue of solidarity, as it is examined and defended here, is based on the recognition that in the violation of another's human rights, my own are at stake. In a real way, the denial of another's human dignity is a denial of my own. Participation in the universal common good and the virtue of solidarity involves the recognition that my own dignity and humanity are at stake, are lessened in the face of human rights violations and oppression. For Christian ethics, this is clearly illustrated through the *imago dei*. Martin Luther King Jr.'s quote at the beginning of this chapter beautifully illustrates this very point, "*I can never be what I ought to be until you are what you ought to be.*"

At the heart of virtue theory is the basic assertion that human beings are always developing; we are becoming what we do. Throughout Catholic social teaching and the Catholic moral tradition, the human person is always called

---

42. David Hollenbach, *Common Good and Christian Ethics* (Cambridge: Cambridge University Press, 2002), 189.

43. Cf. Aquinas, *Summa Theologiae*, IIa IIae.qq 58–122, "Treatise on Justice."

to relationship, called to conversion, and called to develop a more authentically human life. This is the basis for the very ability to acquire virtues as well as our ability to more or less fully image God. Through the virtue of solidarity, we can begin to be more fully what we ought to be. There is no determinism or defeat in Reverend King's statement, but instead there is a recognition that I cannot become more authentically human without an authentically human community and without embracing all authentically common humanity.

For Christian ethics, this does not eliminate or underestimate the reality and prevalence of sin in the world through which "human beings both fall below the possibilities of their own natures in sin and fail to rise to their aspirations to the transcendent good."[44] The virtue of solidarity is not a naive vision of utopia. Instead, it is the recognition that through practicing human rights, as the right kind of actions and emotional reactions, individuals and communities can develop solidarity as a firm and persevering disposition. It is based upon a theological commitment that we are able to become more fully human, more fully who we are. As it becomes a firm and persevering character among individuals and communities—that is, as it becomes an acquired moral social virtue—more substantive human rights will exist. The challenge is to actively aim at the virtue in our various communities while resisting the very seductive and powerful vices of individualism and collectivism in all their incarnations.

---

44. Eileen Sweeney, "Vice and Sin (Ia IIae, qq. 71–89)" in Pope, *Ethics of Aquinas*, 166.

5

Engaging the Future of the Human Rights Project and Building Solidarity

"It is the culture of solidarity that [makes the world more habitable], seeing others not as rivals or statistics, but brothers and sisters."
    Pope Francis, Address to the Community of Varginha[1]

"Because when you truly accept that those children in some far off place in the global village have the same value as you in God's eyes or even in just your eyes, then your life is forever changed, you see something that you can't un-see."
    Bono[2]

Human rights and solidarity emerged as the twin pillars of Catholic social thought in the last fifty years. Elaborating the relationship between human rights and solidarity as grounded in the human person, this book seeks clarifies both the virtue of solidarity and the moral obligations of human rights. Further, through a theological reflection on solidarity and the *imago dei*, I argue that the human person as the living image of God (SRS 40) includes the human community as the living image of the Trinity. This is an integral element of the Christian theological claim that human person is *neighbor*, equally created in the image of God. The human person as created in the image and likeness of the triune God places an ethical claim on us, individually and collectively. But it also requires respect for the fact that, as *imago trinitatis*, we are together

---

1. Francis, "Address of Pope Francis." Visit to the community of Varginha (Manguinhos), Brazil. July 25, 2013,http://www.vatican.va/holy_father/francesco/speeches/2013/july/documents/papa-francesco_20130725_gmg-comunita-varginha_en.html.
    2. Bono, Speech to Global Social Enterprise Initiative (GSEI) at Georgetown's McDonough School of Business, November 12, 2012, http://www.georgetown.edu/webcast/bono-social-enterprise.html.

created in the image and likeness of God. Solidarity, then, is the Christian virtue by which we strive to more fully image God in communion. It is also the virtue by which we live more fully human lives together. What is at stake in debates concerning the moral obligations of human rights is the effectiveness of our witness to the *imago dei*, the dignity of the human person. In solidarity, the dignity at stake is not only that of the vulnerable or victim, but our own dignity as well, our participation in the humanity of each other. The specific requirements of living human rights in solidarity depend on the many capabilities of the human person. The obligation to cultivate the virtue of solidarity through practicing human rights and participating in the universal common good excludes no one. Participation, then, is the method by which we practice human rights in the cultivation of the social virtue of solidarity. Thus, as African moral theologian Jacquineau Azétsop, SJ, notes, "solidarity is both a chance and a risk."[3] This chance or possibility is to live more fully human lives and more fully image God, which "creates an effective space for human flourishing. Solidarity is a risk because it demands the participation of all members in the welfare of the group."[4] This vision is directed both to the church and all people of goodwill. As such, it can focus and contribute practically to the broader discussions on the future of global human rights.

In March 2010, I traveled to Bagaces, Costa Rica, for a weeklong service project with a dozen students and my theology department colleague Dan Daly from Saint Anselm College. Volunteer programs, service learning, and weeklong service trips are now commonplace on American college campuses. These programs offer students powerful opportunities to engage the wider community through experiential learning. Our experience was organized through the Christian Foundation for Children and Aging (CFCA), and we were tasked with building a house for a young immigrant family who were homeless and expecting their second child.[5] Each morning we left our motel around eight o'clock, walked down the street to a local café for breakfast, then headed down a mixture of paved and dirt roads to our building site. Working with some local craftsmen and the husband, we built a concrete house without machines or power tools. The intense physical labor was combined with short breaks playing catch with neighborhood children. When the house

---

3. Jacquineau Azétsop, SJ, and Blondin A. Diop, "Access to Antiretroviral Treatment, Issues of Well-Being and Public Jealth Governance in Chad: What Justifies the Limited Success of the Iniversal Access Policy?," *Philosophy, Ethics, and Humanities in Medicine* 8, no. 8 (2013): 7.

4. Ibid., 7.

5. Since 2010, Christian Foundation for Children and Aging was renamed Unbound. For history and current information see: http://www.unbound.org/

was completed, it would be connected to the electric wires, but it would only be hooked up on our last day when professionals came to install the roof. While most of the people we encountered had their basic needs met, life was a struggle and there was little room for error. The town of Bagaces, in the province of Guanacaste, had widespread relative poverty, with few wealthy people and few facing extreme deprivation.[6] Like many undergraduates, my students were focused on accomplishing their task—they did not want to take breaks and had to be forced to stop for lunch and dinner. This focus on helping and on the particular task is common in volunteer or other human rights work. However, the vision of Catholic social thought calls for a different type of engagement. Success requires more than merely completing the task; it also asks us to build solidarity through practicing human rights.

Each day at lunch, all of the women on the block helped cook the food CFCA provided and prepare lunch. We were invited into their homes and extra tables were set up in the backyard. They welcomed us into their community with their hospitality. We were providing needed labor, but the community invited us to participate in what was their project, not ours. As a community, they had chosen the family and housing site. We were building community with them, not building a house for them. This participation was crucial—it was not enough to bring resources and accomplish our task. Despite the language barrier, we were one community united in the project. Yet, this was the element with which many of my students genuinely struggled. Uncomfortable with taking time or resources from the poor, they often manifested a laser focus on the concrete building task and experienced discomfort at eating the papayas the village women bought for us off the fruit truck. Solidarity, however, requires genuine mutuality and reciprocity in the relationship. I can come in and help you, but if the relationship is not one of mutual participation, then it will not be one of solidarity.

Complete focus on the limited project of building a house provides insulation from the vulnerability, the questions, and the challenge posed by the reality of relative poverty. For Catholic social thought, the elements that

---

6. Extreme poverty is defined by the global poverty line of .25 per day. It is the focus of Millennium Development Goal and is an example of an absolute poverty definition. Relative poverty, on the other hand, focuses on standard of living and scale of deprivation. For more information see "Relative Poverty, Absolute Poverty and Social Exclusion," The Poverty Site, http://www.poverty.org.uk/summary/social exclusion.shtml. "*Absolute poverty* refers to a set standard which is the same in all countries and which does not change over time. An income-related example would be living on less than $X per day. *Relative poverty* refers to a standard which is defined in terms of the society in which an individual lives and which therefore differs between countries and over time."

often make us, as Americans, anxious are absolutely crucial. Those lunches hosted by the women were a major element of what made solidarity possible. Engaging the vulnerability and poverty through solidarity in Bagaces forced us to be vulnerable and to ask difficult questions about poverty in our own communities. Solidarity with those in Bagaces was made possible only through the vulnerability experienced when we realized our humanity is bound up with theirs. That experience generated an opening that draws us into relationship with those in relative poverty back home. Engagement through those lunches pushed us beyond the moral problematic of seeing only what is lacking or of making sharp judgments about the people in poverty we encountered and people facing poverty in our own communities.

Commitment to human rights and solidarity is always grounded in the personal. Responding to human rights violations begins with the recognition of the other as an equal human being. As we respond, in the interplay of these experiences locally and globally, we begin to build solidarity. How do I engage a different context? How do I begin not with poverty but with personhood? As Taylor notes, "Our age makes higher demands of solidarity and benevolence on people today than ever before. Never before have people been asked to stretch so far and so consistently, so systematically, so as a matter of course, to the stranger outside the gates."[7] Yet, practicing this level of solidarity is incredibly difficult. Building solidarity and practicing human rights requires seeing the people in front of me first. Only then can I move to the injustice of poverty. Solidarity and substantive human rights are realized through human encounter and not through the abstract. It is a challenge, however, to see persons, not poverty, as the necessary starting point.

At one point in our trip as we were walking home, a group of children from a different neighborhood swarmed us looking for stuff—footballs, Frisbees, stickers, and so on. The situation was upsetting and problematic from every angle. Motivated by generosity, the students wanted to give the children what they asked for, and yet behind the generosity was a preoccupation with the perception of poverty. In the neighborhood in which we were working, it was different because there was a broader and deeper community relationship involved that created a context for generosity outside of simply the perception of poverty. This was not the case with random children from a different neighborhood following us down the street. "Can I have that?" a small child asks one of our students as we're walking home, pointing first to her camera, then to her bracelet. It was clear that the mother had sent the children out "to the

7. Charles Taylor, *A Secular Age* (Cambridge, MA: Belknap Press of Harvard University Press, 2007), 695.

Americans." And we all struggled with why, in my only assertion as a faculty member, I quickly moved us away from the group. Creating a relationship in which "Americans" come down and hand out stuff, without solidarity, sets up structures of dependency. Broader questions of neocolonialism, racial justice, and social sin on a global scale all complicate the interactions we had with the children we met in Bagaces. But this is not any different from questions of solidarity within our national and local contexts. As we walked away from the family of children following us, I was taken back to my own time as an undergraduate volunteering at St. Ann's afterschool program in the South Bronx. Made famous by Jonathan Kozol's *Amazing Grace*, St. Ann's provides homework help, food, and a safe place to play. As I was helping an eight-year-old African American girl with her math homework, I still remember her looking up at me and saying, "I know you all come down here to help us." At eight, she didn't mean college students, she meant white college students. This is why the question of solidarity as a social virtue, participation, and the structure of our relationships are so important. The relationship between a college student and the child she is tutoring, or between a teacher and members of a weekly CCD class, is not one of equals in power or role, but can be founded on the equality of persons. Thus, if the participants are vulnerable and fully human in the encounter, it can be one that builds solidarity.

My humanity is bound up in yours—this idea is fundamental for the vision of Catholic social thought. I cannot build a relationship of equal human dignity unless I begin from that starting point. If your pain cannot change me and my pain cannot change you, then the relationship cannot be one of solidarity, even if basic needs are being met. For solidarity, as noted in the last chapter, it is not enough to recognize and fight injustice; vulnerability and participation grounded in the one human family must also be present. I must see your dignity bound up with mine. Without that vulnerability and participation, motivation for basic human rights becomes more and more difficult. This sad reality is powerfully demonstrated by the international response to the Rwandan genocide and hauntingly depicted the movie *Hotel Rwanda*. Upon news that coverage will run on international news, the hotel manager Paul thanks the reporter:

> Paul Rusesabagina: I am glad that you have shot this footage and that the world will see it. It is the only way we have a chance that people might intervene.
> Jack: Yeah and if no one intervenes, is it still a good thing to show?

> Paul Rusesabagina: How can they not intervene when they witness such atrocities?
>
> Jack: I think if people see this footage they'll say, "oh my God that's horrible," and then go on eating their dinners.[8]

Unfortunately, the reporter was right. Seeing and knowing about an ongoing genocide was not sufficient to prompt action. Even today it is not sufficient to motivate sustained focus to determine a proper course of action, as long-term humanitarian crises like Darfur have shown. The horror of injustice by itself has not proven sufficient motivation. Common humanity must be the starting point understood through radical interdependence. Catholic social thought offers an understanding of human persons in community in which human dignity is always both personal and universal. My dignity is bound up in yours, and mine is attacked where yours is attacked—this challenges hard distinctions between *us* and *them*. Christian popular music artist Sara Groves, inspired by a mission trip to Rwanda, wrote the powerful "I Saw What I Saw." We played this song during reflection in Costa Rica. Her poignant expression, about the deeply human encounter that cut to the core of how she understood the world, captures what it means for our humanity to be bound up together. She movingly portrays the vulnerability and solidarity in which *"your pain has changed me,"* and she recognizes, as Bono highlighted in his address to Georgetown University, that once one recognizes the humanity in the other, one has seen something that cannot be unseen.[9] In this radical encounter where one sees the victims of injustice as brothers and sisters, solidarity is possible and substantive exercise of human rights attainable. The virtue of solidarity and the praxis of human rights require your pain to change me. Participation in the humanity of one another is necessary.

Building solidarity through human rights requires equality, mutuality, and reciprocity as prerequisites. As we saw in chapter 2, the model against which Catholic social thought judges this is the Trinity. Solidarity cannot fully occur unless there is true human participation in which we are all human, vulnerable, and engaged in the encounter. As argued in the last chapter, solidarity cannot be

---

8. Keir Pearson and Terry George, "Hotel Rwanda," script, quote taken from: "They Do Not Care," Real American History, Films: Hotel Rwanda: Key Passages. http://www.digital.lib.lehigh.edu/trial/reels/films/list/0_53_4 more on Paul Rusesabagina see "Paul Rusesabagina, No 'Ordinary Man,'" NPR, April 6, 2006, http://www.npr.org/2006/04/06/5324187/paul-rusesabagina-no-ordinary-man; and Hotel Rwanda Rusesabagina Foundation, http://hrrfoundation.org/.

9. Sara Groves, "I Saw What I Saw," http://www.saragroves.com/ Lyrics found at songlyrics.com/sara-groves-I-saw-what-I-saw

one-sided; however, neither can human rights. The two are intimately linked in our one humanity shared by all. As the 2013 Bangladesh factory collapses horrifyingly remind us, the choices I make in a New York clothing store reverberate in towns and villages across the world. Responding to the atrocity of human trafficking, Pope Francis lamented, "In a world that talks so much about rights, how many times are human rights trampled. . . . In a world that talks so much about rights, the only thing that seems to have them is money."[10] Imbalances of power and human rights call out for our attention. The economic vices detailed in chapter 4 reinforce these imbalances and create deep social vices clouding the humanity of the other. The interdependence of the one human family and human rights abuses around the world prompt us to reexamine the future of the human rights project and building solidarity. Practically, on a global level this raises questions about power, agency, and the need to rethink responsibility for human rights in light of globalization. In particular, how do we structure development aid based upon solidarity and human rights? How do we adequately account for transnational actors? What do we owe distant populations? Do we have a *responsibility to protect* peoples from genocide, displacement, and other crimes against humanity? How can we build partnerships of solidarity? The integrated vision of Catholic social thought provides an ethical framework from which to approach these questions—using the virtue of solidarity and the praxis of human rights addressed to all people of goodwill. Human rights and solidarity are two sides of the same coin, two irreducible elements of who we are as persons. Truly seeking to unite the local and global, Catholic social thought understands the virtue of solidarity as possible in individuals, communities, and nation-states, and offers a substantive way to expand our understanding of obligations beyond the paradigm of individuals and nation-states. As such, I contend it can significantly contribute to these ongoing global conversations through its understanding of solidarity and human rights. Pushing beyond simply legal conversations into ethical norms and imagination, Catholic social thought establishes guidelines for solidarity and human rights that appreciate human diversity and also begin with the affirmation that "*we're one but we're not the same. We get to carry each other*" ("One," by U2).

10. Francis, quoted in Cindy Wooden, Pope Calls Human Trafficking 'Despicable, a Disgrace,'" *Catholic News Service*, May 24, 2013, http://www.catholicnews.com/data/stories/cns/1302314.htm.

RETHINKING RESPONSIBILITY FOR HUMAN RIGHTS

Traditionally, human rights practice focuses on the individuals who are the bearers of these rights and the nation-state from whom the individual claims these rights. In this framework, it is the nation-state and, globally, the community of nations (that is, the United Nations, European Union, African Union) who have the duty or obligation to protect and promote these rights. The relationship between institutions as agents of justice is intimately connected to the participation of individuals and individual agency, as individual capabilities and agency only develop with a great deal of institutional and social support. Reiterating the basic insight of Sen examined in chapter 3, philosopher Onora O'Neill explains, "Agents and agencies can only be obliged to act in ways for which they have an adequate set of capabilities. Where there is an effective primary agent of justice, the allocation of specific obligations to other agents and agencies with coherent and effective capabilities to discharge them is feasible."[11] Without diminishing the civil authority's responsibility, the realities of transnational corporations and globalization have prompted many philosophers and activists to begin asking what the responsibilities of transnational actors are. O'Neill questions the continued relevance and practicality of locating the obligations or responsibilities of global justice and human rights entirely within the state. She highlights an inconsistency in examining the role of states and other agents of justice, pointing out, "One example is the *Universal Declaration* of 1948, which demands 'the promotion of universal respect for and observance of human rights,' then assumes that this noble goal can be pursued by assigning to states the counterpart obligations to respect these rights."[12] In this view, the state is the primary agent of justice and insufficient attention is paid to secondary agents of justice. States are not always capable of fulfilling or willing to fulfill the obligations of human rights: some are unjust, some are simply unable to secure human rights for their citizens, and "even states with some capacities to secure rights, and in particular the rights of their own citizens, often find that processes of globalization require them to make their borders more porous, thereby weakening state power and allowing powerful agents and agencies of other sorts to become more active within their borders."[13]

Cosmopolitan philosophers and human rights activists seek to expand the categories of agents of justice to incorporate a more robust theory of secondary

---

11. Onora O'Neill, "Global Justice: Whose Obligations?," in *The Ethics of Assistance: Morality and the Distant Needy*, ed. Deen K. Chatterjee (Cambridge: Cambridge University Press, 2004), p. 250.

12. Ibid.243.

13. Ibid, 247.

actors. In examining the relationship between *ought* and *can*, O'Neill identifies the need to expand who counts as an agent of justice. Given globalization, it is necessary to expand the role of traditional *secondary agents of justice* because, in many cases, these secondary agents, such as nongovernmental organizations (NGOs), transnational corporations (TNCs), and transnational networks, may be better equipped as agents of justice than the state. The capability to enhance substantive freedoms and promote human rights, for O'Neill, corresponds to an obligation to do just that.[14] Where nonstate actors can contribute to justice, fundamental obligations that in other circumstances are secured by compliance with state requirements demand that they do so. If we take rights to be universal, we need to look realistically at actual agents and agencies, with their actual powers and vulnerabilities. We need not assume that nonstate actors will be paralyzed in weak states or that all progress to justice must be endlessly postponed until more competent and just states emerge.[15]

In addition to rethinking responsibility to include transnational actors, a broader approach to duties and obligations that include individuals, professions, and institutions is needed. Two prominent thinkers, philosopher Thomas Pogge and physician and anthropologist Paul Farmer, offer arguments for including structural and institutional aspects in the analysis of who bears responsibility for human rights.[16] Rethinking responsibility for financing human rights development, Thomas Pogge focuses on levels of duties and obligations with respect to human rights. He argues that, beyond the nation-state, individuals as citizens bear duties and obligations to respect, promote, and protect human rights. As citizens, Pogge explains, we have two obligations: "One of these derives from their quite general positive duty to promote the justice of social institutions for the sake of safeguarding the rights and needs of human beings anywhere. The other obligation derives from their negative duty not to collaborate in designing or imposing unjust social institutions upon other human beings."[17] While Pogge focuses on citizenship and then broadens

14. Ibid, 252–56.

15. Ibid, 258.

16. In the topic of the obligations of human rights, cf. also Thomas Pogge, "Assisting the Global Poor," in Chatterjee, *The Ethics of Assistance*; Thomas Pogge, *World Poverty and Human Rights: Cosmopolitan Responsibilities and Reforms* (Cambridge, UK: Polity, 2002); and Thomas Pogge, "Poverty and Human Rights" n.d., available at the website of the UN Office of the High Commissioner for Human Rights, http://www2.ohchr.org/english/issues/poverty/expert/docs/Thomas_Pogge_Summary.pdf. See also Rowan Cruft, "Human Rights and Positive Duties," response to *World Poverty and Human Rights*, by Thomas Pogge, *Ethics & International Affairs* 19, no. 1 (2006); and Paul Farmer, *Pathologies of Power: Health, Human Rights and the New War on the Poor* (Berkeley: University of California Press, 2005).

obligations to humanity, the vision of Catholic social thought detailed in the previous four chapters offers a framework that begins not with citizenship but with the simultaneous principles of equal human dignity of each human person and the one human family.

Similarly, Paul Farmer examines the practice of global health and medicine from the perspective of human rights, using the concept of structural violence "as a broad rubric that includes a host of offences against human dignity: extreme and relative poverty, social inequalities ranging from racism to gender inequality, and the more spectacular forms of violence that are uncontestedly human rights abuses."[18] In using this concept, Farmer attempts "to identify the forces conspiring to promote suffering, to discern the causes of extreme suffering and also the forces that put some at risk for human rights abuses, while others are shielded from risk."[19] Like Pogge, Farmer is pushing the questions back upon those citizens and medical professionals of wealthy countries to examine what shields them from harm while others are in perpetual vulnerability. Influenced by Catholic theology and solidarity, Farmer's work on global health and human rights through Partners in Health emphasizes working with the poor and vulnerable through participation and accompaniment.[20] The focus on institutions and social structures is shared with Catholic social thought. In this diverse conversation about transnational actors and responsibility for human rights, the vision of Catholic social thought provides support and clarification.

In 1963 when *Pacem in Terris* was released, Pope John XXIII was critiqued for being naive and overly optimistic. In that document, he envisioned a global institution of an order that has never existed—the United Nations was not commissioned as such. And yet, in what appeared as folly to many, *Pacem in Terris* gave us a beautiful gift. Human rights as they are developed in Catholic social teaching operate on all levels of society—there are rights and responsibilities for individuals, communities, societies, and the one human family. Enforcement aside, *Pacem in Terris* established a Catholic human rights tradition that pushed beyond the limits of the nation-state model. In an era of globalization and transnational actors, this broader understanding of human rights and communities provides resources for developing the theory and practices for secondary agents of justice. If solidarity and human rights are both

17. Thomas Pogge, "Are We Violating the Human Rights of the World's Poor?," *Yale Human Rights and Development Law Journal* 14, no. 2 (2012), 16.

18. Paul Farmer, *Pathologies of Power*, 8.

19. Ibid., 50.

20. "Our Mission," Partners in Health, http://www.pih.org/pages/our-mission.

grounded in the human person, as detailed throughout the previous chapters, then no individual or institution is automatically exempt from the obligations of human rights. The scope of obligations for human rights emerges precisely in solidarity. Human rights are a matter of who we are as human persons. Because of our common humanity, we ought to practice respect for those rights not only for ourselves but for all human persons; in this focus on the one human family together, we can possibly achieve this and make possible building a community with the social virtue of solidarity. Specific responsibilities are complicated and contextual, as chapter 3 indicated, and ethical frameworks like the Kew Gardens Principles highlight that reality. The question of *can* and *ought* must be asked on the individual and communal levels when faced with particular human rights violations; however, part of rethinking responsibility for human rights in light of solidarity highlights the universal ethical claim they place on the one human family.

Without diminishing the practical obligations of nation–states in promoting and respecting the human rights of their citizens, the virtue of solidarity prevents limiting human rights responsibilities to the state alone. Furthermore, if the end of the virtue of solidarity is participation in the universal common good, then all levels of community have an obligation to cultivate this virtue through the praxis of human rights to the extent that their situation and capabilities allow. Built into the vision of Catholic social thought is a framework where each of us must examine how we can practice human rights and cultivate solidarity. Framed as a moral question, the limit of our responsibility is not legal but, as Taylor understands the modern moral order, is one of creating a civilization of human rights. Catholic social teaching's virtue of solidarity not only points the conversation to a question of capability, but also reminds us that participation on all sides is required in order to have both authentic human rights and solidarity. Any new conception of the moral obligations of human rights must reflect agency and participation by states, NGOs, TNCs, communities, and individual agents, including those whose rights are exploited, violated, and denigrated. The goal is the virtue of solidarity and the means by which it is cultivated by individual communities or transnational movements is through practicing respect for human rights. Since his installation as pope, Francis has repeatedly made public statements to this effect—regarding slave labor, human trafficking, and other corporate practices that violate human dignity.

Participation in Catholic social thought offers a necessary critique of global structures that fail to have a strong determinative voice for developing peoples. Beginning with the one human family, human rights exert a perpetual claim against power structures based on wealth and influence. This claim is visible through the lens of solidarity, the virtue opposed to the capitalistic mechanism and laissez-faire capitalism, as well as the other vices of extreme individualism or collectivism examined in the previous chapter. With the community as a locus for moral analysis, the virtue of solidarity provides a way of approaching the complexities of responsibility in different contexts. Moving beyond purely negative obligations, the vision of Catholic social thought provides a method for evaluating action. Instead of Kant's universalizability as the frame for responsibility, Catholic social thought relies on an objective yet circumstantial method built on the philosophy of Aquinas. Beginning with the objective moral wrong of human rights violations, the moral analysis detailed in chapter 4 helps determine our positive responsibilities in a particular case through the principles of participation, equality, and reciprocity.

THE RESPONSIBILITY TO PROTECT AND SOLIDARITY

A second, yet related, area of emerging human rights discourse to which the vision of Catholic social thought can contribute is the *responsibility to protect* movement. Developed in response to horrors such as the Rwandan genocide, the responsibility to protect is an attempt to develop systematic criteria and structures to guide a response to mass human rights violations by a state against its own people. First articulated by the International Commission on Intervention and State Sovereignty (ICISS), the *responsibility to protect*, or RtoP, reorients the traditional understanding of state sovereignty, which focused on the state's right to noninterference.[21] The proper role of the state, ICISS notes, is to protect its own people, and it is in this obligation that the boundaries of sovereignty emerge. In 2005, the United Nations World Summit affirmed RtoP as grounded on "three equally weighted and nonsequential pillars: (1) The primary responsibility of states to protect their own populations from the four crimes of genocide, war crimes, ethnic cleansing, and crimes against humanity, as well as from their incitement; (2) the international community's responsibility to assist a state to fulfill its RtoP; and (3) the international community's responsibility to take timely and decisive action in accordance with the UN Charter, in cases where the state has manifestly failed to protect its population."[22] The vision established by these three pillars is one of a primarily supportive relationship between individual states and the international

---

21. World Federalist Movement, Institute for Global Policy, "Summary of *Responsibility to Protect*: The Report of the International Commission on Intervention and State Sovereignty (ICISS)," Responsibility to Protect—Engaging Civil Society, http://www.responsibilitytoprotect.org/files/R2PSummary.pdf.

community. Both the primary responsibility of the state and the role of the international community for human rights are included in the obligations of the one human family. The responsibility to protect is a fundamental obligation of all states; therefore, it is not a matter of application but implementation, as Secretary General Ban Ki-Moon has emphasized in his UN agenda. RtoP always applies, even to states without human rights crises, but implementation and responsibility for implementation are the key questions. The proper question is not whether RtoP applies but how we implement this protocol.[23] In a manner similar to the philosophical debate concerning the locus of responsibility, the United Nations and international community raise the question of moral obligation for human rights. The Universal Declaration of Human Rights delineates a set of moral rights to be universally applied to all human persons as well as all legal persons. This requires obligations that extend beyond the nation-state. The ICISS council concludes that "the debate about intervention for human protection purposes should focus not on the 'right to intervene' but on the 'responsibility to protect.' . . . [T]he responsibility to protect implies an evaluation of the [human rights] issues from the point of view of those seeking or needing support, rather than those who may be considering intervention."[24]

As it is emerging, RtoP is an attempt by the international community to create a moral and practical framework based on human rights and interdependence as moral categories. In his 2008 speech to the United Nations, Pope Benedict XVI applauds the fact that the "recognition of the unity of the human family, and attention to the innate dignity of every man and woman, today find renewed emphasis in the principle of the responsibility to protect. . . . What is needed is a deeper search for ways of pre-empting and managing conflicts by exploring every possible diplomatic avenue and giving attention and encouragement to even the faintest sign of dialogue or desire for reconciliation."[25] While acknowledging the need for uniform standards for responding to atrocities, the RtoP pillars place equal emphasis on assisting and supporting states' own implementation of RtoP. Evaluating the first five

22. Alex J. Bellamy, "The Responsibility to Protect—Five Years On," *Ethics & International Affairs* 24, no. 2 (2010): 143, summarized from the UN General Assembly, "2005 World Summit Outcome," para. 138–40.

23. UN General Assembly, "Implementing the Responsibility to Protect: Report of the Secretary General," January 12, 2009, http://responsibilitytoprotect.org/implementing the rtop.pdf.

24. World Federalist Movement, Institute for Global Policy, "Summary of *Responsibility to Protect:* The Report of the International Commission on Intervention and State Sovereignty (ICISS)," Responsibility to Protect—Engaging Civil Society, http://www.responsibilitytoprotect.org/files/R2PSummary.pdf3 (para 2.29 of full report).

years of RtoP, political scientist Alex Bellamy emphasizes that this is still an emerging international norm. The vision of Catholic social thought offers a concrete focus on participation to the development of RtoP. Participation of those in jeopardy is essential for the justification and explanation of the responsibility to protect. This emerging principle, still the subject of much debate and clarification within the international political and intellectual community, is a clear instance of the unavoidable interaction between solidarity and human rights. At the conclusion of *The Challenge of Human Rights*, Jack Mahoney, SJ, states, "For what the existence of human rights reveals is human solidarity. . . . More than that, we can now conclude that human rights constitute of the single human race a single moral family."[26] The emerging responsibility to protect is a practical example of this—human rights revealing human solidarity.

The philosophical and theological levels of solidarity, culminating with the virtue of solidarity delineated in the previous chapter, focus on solidarity as both descriptive and normative. As such, that which illuminates solidarity as a descriptive element of humanity also enhances our understanding of human rights. In the emerging principle of the responsibility to protect, the connection between the two is clearly revealed. The emphasis on participation and agency on the part of the vulnerable population, in both the responsibility to protect and practices surrounding the protection of the human rights of refugees, broadens our understanding of individual human rights, substantive freedom, and the role of the community.[27] In this ongoing conversation, the approach to human rights and solidarity in Catholic social teaching provides insights and support for the United Nations and for the world's development of a more integrated approach to human rights that necessarily includes solidarity. The necessary relationship between the two can contribute to strengthening the purpose and theoretical argument for the responsibility to protect. Once again, Catholic social thought provides an understanding of the person and moral framework that has a rich and complex understanding of community which includes but is not limited to the nation-state. The moral vision of Catholic social thought, therefore, provides resources for all people of goodwill engaged in reframing sovereignty and the role of the international community

25. Pope Benedict XIV, Address to the United Nations General Assembly, April 18, 2008, http://www.vatican.va/holy_father/benedict_xvi/speeches/2008/april/documents/hf_ben-xvi_spe_20080418_un-visit_en.html.

26. Jack Mahoney, SJ, *The Challenge of Human Rights*, 187.

27. UNHCR, *Protecting Refugees and the Role of the UNHCR, 2007–2008* (Geneva: UNHCR, 2007), http://www.unhcr.org/49eecf142.html.

in implementing human rights and creating a method for responding to situations of mass atrocities. As chapter 3 indicates, a more integrated approach to human rights has begun to be implemented in the area of development with the Millennium Development Goals, which in turn provide concrete data supporting a holistic approach similar to that offered by Catholic social teaching. This richer understanding of human rights and solidarity can also provide resources for the development of RtoP, questions of peace building, and responses to violence.

Partnerships for Solidarity and Millennium Development Goals: The Example of the Sudan National Helping Babies Breathe Initiative (MDG 4)

The Millennium Development Goals and the UNDP Human Development Reports were highlighted in chapter 3 as providing concrete data supporting some of the integral human development claims of Catholic social thought. The international community is moving progressively toward an understanding of human rights in practice that focuses more on the community, providing practical examples of effective human rights praxis leading to strong communities and the possibility of solidarity. The vision of Catholic social thought provides a framework for evaluating these programs and partnerships for their emphasis on participation and solidarity. As the example from Costa Rica indicates, human rights praxis must begin with the realization that we are one human family and that violations of another's rights are an attack on mine as well. Starting with the human person in this way—as Catholic social teaching does—participation emerges as the primary moral principle for evaluating partnerships. A main question for Catholic social thought and human development projects is whether or not solidarity can be cultivated on an international scale. For this to be possible, active participation, as detailed in chapter 4, must be present in the establishing, executing, and future planning of projects, as well as in the process of incorporating all of the stakeholders in the particular community. Is it possible to have true participation across class and cultural divides? Can we have just partnerships focused on human rights that lead to solidarity? Catholic social thought holds that this is possible, that solidarity on both local and global scales is a possibility if we are all fully human in the relationship. What would that require? It requires an engagement that is substantive, not procedural. The difference is perhaps best explained through a case study. In January 2013, I accompanied the Sudan Helping Babies Breathe (HBB) National Initiative to Khartoum, Sudan.[28] This particular international partnership demonstrated lessons for how to model participation as well as warnings about how power can influence the active participation of others. With participation as the key, practicing respect for human rights can cultivate solidarity. Furthermore, through the lessons of the Sudanese HBB National Initiative, it is clear that this participation is necessary for the very effectiveness of human rights partnerships themselves.

Millennium Development Goal 4: Reduce Child Mortality established the goal of cutting the 1990 mortality rate for children under five by two-thirds. According to the United Nations, great progress has been made in the last decade, "which translates into about 14,000 fewer children dying each day."[29] Despite Africa accounting for only 17 percent of births, 40 percent of deaths of children under five years old occur there.[30] Monitoring of progress toward the goal revealed that, despite gains, "an increasing proportion of under-5 deaths occur in the neonatal period or the first 28 days after birth."[31] According to *State of the World's Children: Maternal and Newborn Health*, UNICEF estimates that "between 25 and 45 percent of neonatal deaths" occur within the first day of life.[32] An astounding 98 percent of these deaths occur within low-resource and less-developed countries.[33] Thirty-four of the thirty-eight countries that continue to have under-five mortality greater than 80 per 1,000 births are concentrated in the sub-Saharan region of Africa.[34] In these countries, births

28. I observed the trainings and spoke with instructors, participants, and other health professionals during the week in Khartoum. This ethics analysis would not have been possible without the permission and cooperation of Dr. C. A. Ryan (Ireland), Dr. Sami Ahmed (Ireland), Dr. Abdelomoniem (Sudan), and Dr. Lisa McCarthy-Clark (United States). Thank you also to Sister-Nurse Hind Waly (Sudan) at the CPD center for assistance on-site and in translation. This ethics fieldwork was also made possible by a Summer Support of Research Grant from St. John's University.

29. "Goal 4: Reduce Child Mortality," UN Millennium Development Goals, http://www.un.org/millenniumgoals/childhealth.shtml.

30. Government of Sudan, Federal Ministry of Health, Primary Health Care General Directorate, Mother and Child Health Directorate, "Road Map for Reducing Maternal and Newborn Mortality in Sudan (2010–2015)," December 2009; submitted to UNFPA by the Sudanese government, http://www.unfpa.org/sowmy/resources/docs/library/R101_MOHSudan_2010_MNMR_RoadMap_06Jan10.doc.

31. George A. Little et al., "Neonatal Nursing and Helping Babies Breathe: An Effective Intervention to Decrease Global Neonatal Mortality," *Pediatrics* 126, no. 5 (2010): 82–83, http://www.helpingbabiesbreathe.org/docs/Neonatal Nursing 2011.pdf.See also: S. Wall, et al.,"Neonatal Resuscitation in Low-Resource Settings: What, Who, and How to Overcome Challenges to Scale Up?," *International Journal of Gynecology & Obstetrics* 107, suppl. (October 2009): S47–S64.

32. UNICEF, State of the World's Children 2009, http://www.unicef.org/protection/SOWC09-FullReport-EN.pdf.

33. Little et al., "Neonatal Nursing," 82.

are often attended by only one or no skilled birth attendants responsible for both the mother and baby, and neonatal mortality rates are higher in rural areas within developing countries. Newborn death remains a major global health and human rights concern.[35] In response, the American Academy of Pediatrics, the U.S. Agency for International Development (USAID), the World Health Organization (WHO), Save the Children, Laerdal, and others developed an evidence-based education program for low-resource settings called Helping Babies Breathe (HBB), launched in 2010.[36] HBB is a training program for midwives and skilled birth attendants in basic neonatal care, including resuscitation using a *bag and mask* and is structured as a participatory learning experience around simulations and practical skills. HBB focuses on actions during the first sixty seconds, which can drastically reduce mortality and morbidity. Sudan is one of the nations with significant neonatal mortality. The last Sudan Household Survey (2006) approved by the government placed infant mortality at 81 per 1,000 births and neonatal mortality at 41 per 1,000 births.[37] Thus, Sudan is HBB's target audience. It has high neonatal mortality and 80 percent of births take place outside of hospital or clinics.[38]

The Sudan HBB National Initiative emerged out of a long-standing partnership between Omdurman Maternity Hospital (Khartoum) and Cork University Maternity Hospital (Cork, Ireland) that enriched both programs focusing on maternal mortality and stillbirths.[39] The alliance, as it emerged, received approval for good governance from the European ESTHER alliance, which is a cooperative directed to solidarity-based hospital alliances. The Cork-Omdurman partnership was the second ESTHER-approved development program in Ireland (2013).[40] Given the specifics of Sudan's public health and in collaboration with Dr. Abdelmoniem and Sudan's Continuing Professional

34. Julie Knoll Rajaratnam et al., "Neonatal, Postnatal, Childhood, and Under-5 Mortality for 187 Countries, 1970–2010: A Systematic Analysis of Progress towards Millennium Development Goal 4," *Lancet* 375 (2010), doi: 10.1016/S0140-6736(10)60703-9.

35. The World Health Organization estimates "one million babies die each year from birth asphyxia (inability to breathe immediately after delivery)." WHO, "Mortality and Burdens of Disease," World Health Statistics 2009, http://www.who.int/whosis/whostat/EN_WHS09_Table1.pdf.

36. "About Helping Babies Breathe," Helping Babies Breathe, American Academy of Pediatrics, http://www.helpingbabiesbreathe.org/about.html.

37. "Sudan Household Health Survey" UNICEF, 2006, http://www.unicef.org/sudan/health_4284.html, and Government of Sudan, "Road Map for Reducing Maternal and Newborn Mortality in Sudan."

38. The institutional birth rate is 19.7 percent. Government of Sudan, "Road Map for Reducing Maternal and Newborn Mortality in Sudan."

39. Cork-Omdurman Partnership Project, http://www.ucc.ie/cgd/ReportSections/s4-cork.pdf

Development (CPD) centers, a national plan centered on the village midwives was developed out of the Cork-Omdurman partnership. The creation of the Cork-Omdurman partnership and the Sudan HBB National Initiative was participatory from the beginning with Sudanese health experts as a significant driving force of the program. Over two years of planning, a national program was developed that involved the Ministry of Health (at the federal level and in the state of Khartoum) to ensure national participation, including doctors and midwives from rural and conflict regions of Sudan. This government and institutional support was also necessary to secure entry and exit visas for the international training team. Participation in planning the program is a necessary precondition for international human rights partnerships. Without participation at the start, there is little hope for a partnership that meets the actual needs of the people and is sufficiently attentive to their context. It is not enough to diagnose neonatal mortality as a problem. That it is a clear health and human rights concern does not provide a broad enough understanding of the causes to develop a response.

The program itself was structured in two course programs—an English-speaking master trainer's course and an Arabic-speaking trainer's course overseen by an international team of six medical and nursing educators from Ireland and the United States. Each course lasted two days, and all participants received an Arabic HBB flip chart, Laerdal HBB training doll kit, bag and mask, and learner workbook. The first English-speaking master trainer's course was made up of doctors, nurses, and health educators from around Sudan, and students from this course were chosen as the instructors for the second Arabic-speaking course. From the outset, the structure was designed to move quickly, with support for the transition, from instruction by the international team to instruction by Sudanese participants. Participation by all in this kind of educational endeavor is a challenge as power and social dynamics can often present barriers to participation; however, it can be achieved. One clear example of active participation based in mutuality and reciprocity was the invitation of Sudanese public health experts to lead segments of the program, even though they were also participants in the training. The international team was made up of experts in neonatal resuscitation and newborn care, but they were not experts in Sudanese health care, culture, or history. The instructors, then, needed to be open to learning from the Sudanese participants in order for active participation to occur and solidarity to be possible. This occurred in

40. "The European ESTHER Alliance," http://www.esther.eu/, and European ESTHER Alliance, "Charter," http://www.esther.fr/wp-content/uploads/2012/03/Final-Charter-Quality-of-Partnerships_AEE.pdf.

handling the procedures for cleaning and infection control. While the WHO/HBB program has cleaning guidelines, this protocol does not necessarily reflect the available resources in a particular context. Instead of having international experts provide instruction based on a "one size fits all" cleaning protocol, a sister-midwife, who was pursuing a doctorate specializing in infection control, was invited to offer the presentation. Through her participation, she instructed not only her fellow participants but also the international team on the protocols and available resources within Sudan for cleaning and infection control. This is a positive example of the vulnerability and engagement required for true participation. If those from the developed world enter into partnerships for human rights in which they are coming to "bring human rights" to the other without being open to learning, then the partnership cannot ever be one of solidarity.

Solidarity and equal human rights both depend on a truly human encounter based upon the equal dignity of all involved, such as that generated by the hospitality offered to my students and me in Costa Rica. A perpetual danger in international human rights partnerships is the tendency to only see the deprivation, the problem, and look past the contribution of the people involved. All of the Sudanese participants strongly resisted the elements of the HBB materials that assumed a lower-resource setting than they have. For example, since it is a global protocol, HBB does not mandate clamps to tie off the umbilical cord; however, these are available to the rural midwives in Sudan. It takes away from their dignity and substantive exercise of human rights to assume and take away resources to which they do have access. The commitment to human rights and solidarity begins with listening as the first step. As Paul Farmer notes, "To those in great need, solidarity without the pragmatic component can seem like so much abstract piety."[41] Listening to the other is constitutive for participation and partnership for human rights. For the vision of Catholic social thought, solidarity "is not a feeling of vague compassion or shallow distress at the misfortunes of so many people, both near and far. On the contrary, it is a *firm and persevering determination* to commit oneself to the *common good*; that is to say to the good of all and of each individual because we are really *all* responsible *for all*" (SRS 39).

Pragmatic solidarity requires engagement in which both parties are open to question and learning from the other. For international global health partnerships, this requires embracing ambiguity and difference. This challenges human rights activists and global health experts to be vulnerable and experience

41. Farmer, *Pathologies of Power*, 146.

the complexities of different contexts. In Sudan, this difficulty became apparent when village midwives challenged an aspect of the HBB protocol—how and when to cut the umbilical cord. In recent years the World Health Organization changed its recommendation, based on an emerging review of the data, from immediate cutting to delayed cutting (one to three minutes) to increase blood to the newborn. The village midwives, who milked the cord to deliver more blood to the baby, wanted a clear understanding of how and why delayed cutting was better than their practice. Without that argument at hand, *evidence-based medicine* was the fallback for why they should change their practice. The research, however, is inconclusive on whether waiting provides a significantly different outcome from the Sudanese midwives' traditional practice of milking the cord.[42]

Participation involving equality of persons and reciprocity is required for solidarity. Evidence-based medicine is necessary for public health protocols and a systematic approach to health and human rights. Despite its importance, medicine is a perpetually developing field and current protocols cannot be simply taken a priori. Changes in traditional practices must be engaged from below, and engagement rather than uniformity should be the priority. In the case of cutting umbilical cords, the difference between practices is unknown, and, at its worst, even if delayed cutting is of greater benefit, milking the cord is itself a harmless practice. The stakes are significantly higher, however, when the practices human rights activists and global health workers are trying to change are harmful, such as female genital mutilation.

---

42. For more information on the debate, see World Health Organization, "Care of the Cord: Review of the Evidence," 1999, ; E. Abalos, "Effect of Timing of Umbilical Cord Clamping of Term Infants on Maternal and Neonatal Outcomes: RHL Commentary" last revised March 2, 2009, *WHO Reproductive Health Library* (Geneva: World Health Organization), http://apps.who.int/rhl/pregnancy_childbirth/childbirth/3rd_stage/cd004074_abalose_com/en/; H. Rabe et al., "Effect of Timing of Umbilical Cord Clamping and Other Strategies to Influence Placental Transfusion at Preterm Birth on Maternal and Infant Outcomes (Review)," *Cochrane Library*, issue 8 (August 15, 2012), http://onlinelibrary.wiley.com/doi/10.1002/14651858.CD003248.pub3/pdf; A. Upadhyay et al., "Effect of Umbilical Cord Milking in Term and Near Term Infants: Randomized Control Trial," *American Journal of Obstetrics and Gynecology* 208, no. 2 (2013): 120.e1–6, doi: 10.1016/j.ajog.2012.10.884; "Timing of Umbilical Cord Clamping after Birth," Committee Opinion 543, American College of Obstetricians and Gynecologists, *Obstetrics and Gynecology* 120 (2012): 1522–26, http://www.acog.org/Resources And Publications/Committee Opinions/Committee on Obstetric Practice/Timing of Umbilical Cord Clamping After Birth.aspx/

CONCLUSION

As this book was being written, Pope Francis, the first pope from the global South, was elected. While he has not yet added to Catholic social teaching, in the first six months of his papacy, Pope Francis has continually emphasized the moral implications of human rights and solidarity through the attention to those on the margins in his speeches and those with whom he visits. The heart of his message is the radical, uncompromising, and uncomfortable nature of solidarity. In his visit to Lampedusa, he lamented that "in this world of globalization we have fallen into a globalization of indifference. We are accustomed to the suffering of others, it doesn't concern us, it's none of our business."[43] The inability to hear the cries of our neighbor is profoundly dangerous not only for those who have been victims of violent and unrelenting poverty and suffering, like the residents of Lampedusa, but for all of us. Indifference to the humanity of others makes solidarity impossible, but it also makes living a fully human life as an individual impossible, even in a situation of comfort. I cannot embrace my own humanity fully if I do not embrace the humanity of my neighbor who is excluded and marginalized. Pope Francis elaborated on this theme in his visit to the community of Varginha in Brazil stating, "No amount of 'peace-building' will be able to last, nor will harmony and happiness be attained in a society that ignores, pushes to the margins or excludes a part of itself. A society of that kind simply impoverishes itself, it loses something essential. . . . We must never allow the throwaway culture to enter our hearts, because we are brothers and sisters. No one is disposable!"[44] Human rights and solidarity are mutually dependent upon one another; this is a consequence of our humanity.

Similarly, we must resist the temptation to focus on abstract principles or goals in the face of human suffering. Speaking to the Food and Agriculture Organization of the UN, Pope Francis emphasized the centrality of the human person as the locus of human rights, "Our duty is to continue to insist, in the present international context, that the human person and human dignity are not simply catchwords, but pillars for creating shared rules and structures capable of passing beyond purely pragmatic or technical approaches in order to eliminate divisions and to bridge existing differences."[45] Over and over, Pope Francis exposes not only the challenge of solidarity but the ways in which the current

43. Francis (popes do not get I until there is a 2nd.), "The Globalization of Indifference," Address at Lampedusa, July 8, 2013, http://en.radiovaticana.va/news/2013/07/08/pope_on_lampedusa:_"the_globalization_of_indifference"/en1-708541.

44. Francis, "Address of Pope Francis," Community Varginha.

45. Francis, "Address of His Holiness Pope Francis to Participants in the 38th Conference of the Food and Agriculture Organization of the United Nations (FAO)," June 20, 2013, http://www.vatican.va/

global structure fails to meet the requirements of solidarity. Thus, the challenge to rethink responsibility for human rights cuts to the core of both local and global structures. The necessity to integrate human rights in a communal and unified way is also central to the ongoing development agenda of the UN prioritized by Secretary General Ban Ki-Moon. In his report to the sixty-eighth General Assembly, "A Life of Dignity for All: Accelerating Progress towards the Millennium Development Goals and Advancing the United Nations Development Agenda Beyond 2015," the secretary general places this challenge at the heart of the UN agenda. Emphatically stating that the focus of development is persons, he concludes, "No one must be left behind. We must continue to build a future of justice and hope, a life of dignity for all."[46]

My humanity is bound up in yours. The vision of Catholic social thought is grounded in a theological anthropology of a radical unity of the human family. Based on this, solidarity is a social virtue that requires the praxis of human rights. In actively pursuing the justice of human rights, we can habituate solidarity and build community. Pope Francis teaches that we must enter into the humanity of others to fully embrace our own human dignity. To the Jesuit Refugee Service Center in Rome, he elaborates, "To serve means to work alongside the neediest, first of all to establish a close human relationship with them, based on solidarity. Solidarity, this word elicits fear in the developed world. They try not to say it. It's almost a dirty word for them. But it's our word! To serve means to recognize and welcome the demands for justice, for hope, and to seek ways together, a concrete path of liberation."[47] Why does solidarity elicit fear? The answer lies in the struggle of vulnerability, the challenge of facing one's own vulnerability while participating in the reality of others. Solidarity as it has been argued for in this book is uncomfortable, but it is morally necessary if we are to be a truly human community. In line with the call of the gospel, the vision of Catholic social thought invites and challenges us to build a community of solidarity. Human rights are an integral and constitutive element of building this fully human community. A life of dignity for all is at the heart of Catholic social thought's understanding of integral human development and emerges out

holy_father/francesco/speeches/2013/june/documents/papa-francesco_20130620_38-sessione-fao_en.html.

46. Ban Ki-Moon, "A Life of Dignity for All: Accelerating Progress towards the Millennium Development Goals and Advancing the United Nations Development Agenda beyond 2015," United Nations Secretary General's Report, July 26, 2013, 19, http://www.un.org/millenniumgoals/pdf/A Life of Dignity for All.pdf.

47. "Pope Francis' Message to the Jesuit Refugee Service," September 12, 2013, Jesuit Refugee Service USA, http://www.jrsusa.org/news_detail.cfm?TN=NEWS-20130912100648.

of the radical call to build solidarity through living the praxis of human rights together.

Bibliography

Abbey, Ruth, ed. *Charles Taylor*. Contemporary Philosophy in Focus. Cambridge: Cambridge University Press, 2004.

———. "Charles Taylor: Sources of the Self." In *The Twentieth Century: Quine and After*. Central Works of Philosophy, vol. 5, edited by John Shand. Montreal: McGill-Queen's University Press, 2006.

Ake, Claude. "The African Context of Human Rights." In *Applied Ethics: A Multicultural Approach*, edited by Larry May, Shari Collins-Chobanian, and Kai Wong, 94–101. 2nd ed. Upper Saddle River, NJ: Prentice Hall, 1994. Originally published in *Africa Today* 34, no. 142 (1987): 5–13.

Alkire, S. and Santos, M. E. (2013) "Measuring Acute Poverty in the Developing World: Robustness and Scope of the Multidimensional Poverty Index". OPHI Working Paper No 59. http://www.ophi.org.uk/wp-content/uploads/ophi-wp-59.pdf

Alkire, S. and Santos, M.E. (2010) "Acute Multidimensional Poverty: A new index for developing countries," *OPHI Working Paper 38,* UNDP HDRO Background Paper 2010/11 http://www.ophi.org.uk/wp-content/uploads/ophi-wp38.pdf

Alexander, John M. *Capabilities and Social Justice: The Political Philosophy of Amartya Sen and Martha Nussbaum*. Burlington, VT: Ashgate, 2008.

Aquinas, Thomas. *Summa Theologiae*. Allen, TX: Christian Classics, 1991.

Aristotle. *Nichomachean Ethics*. Upper Saddle River, NJ: Prentice Hall, 1999.

Azétsop, Jacquineau, SJ, and Blondin A. Diop. "Access to Antiretroviral Treatment, Issues of Well-Being and Public Health Governance in Chad: What Justifies the Limited Success of the Universal Access Policy?" *Philosophy, Ethics, and Humanities in Medicine* 8, no. 1 (2013): 8.

Baum, Gregory. *Compassion and Solidarity: The Church for Others*. Compassion & Solidarity. New York: Paulist, 1990.

Baum, Gregory, and Robert Ellsberg. *The Logic of Solidarity: Commentaries on Pope John Paul II's encyclical "On Social Concern."* Maryknoll, NY: Orbis, 1989.

Bellamy, Alex J. "The Responsibility to Protect—Five Years On." *Ethics & International Affairs* 24, no. 2 (2010): 143–69.

Benedict XVI, Pope. *Caritas in Veritate.* Encyclical Letter. June 29, 2009. http://www.vatican.va/holy_father/benedict_xvi/encyclicals/documents/ hf_ben-xvi_enc_20090629_caritas-in-veritate_en.html.

———. Address to the United Nations General Assembly. April 18, 2008. http://www.vatican.va/holy_father/benedict_xvi/speeches/2008/april/ documents/hf_ben-xvi_spe_20080418_un-visit_en.html.

———. *Deus Caritas Est.* Encyclical Letter. December 25, 2005. http://www.vatican.va/holy_father/benedict_xvi/encyclicals/documents/ hf_ben-xvi_enc_20051225_deus-caritas-est_en.html.

Berlin, Isaiah, Henry Hardy, and Ian Harris, *Liberty: Incorporating Four Essays on Liberty.* Oxford: Oxford University Press, 2002.

Bilgrien, Marie Vianney, SSND. "Solidarity as a Virtue and the Common Good." In *Foundation Theology 2000: Faculty Essays for Ministry Professionals,* 1–18. Snow Lion Publications. Bristol, IN: Published on behalf of the Graduate Theological Foundation by Wyndham Hall Press, 2000.

Boswell, Jonathan, Francis P. McHugh, and Johan Verstraeten, *Catholic Social Thought: Twilight or Renaissance?* Bibliotheca Ephemeridum Theologicarum Lovaniensium. Louvain: Leuven University Press, 2000.

Botman, H. Russel. "Covenantal Anthropology: Integrating Three Contemporary Discourses of Human Dignity." In *God and Human Dignity,* edited by R. Kendall Soulen and Linda Woodhead, 72–86. Cambridge, UK: Eerdmans, 2006.

Bucar, Elizabeth M., and Barbra Barnett. *Does Human Rights Need God?* Eerdmans Religion, Ethics, and Public Life Series. Grand Rapids, MI: Eerdmans, 2005.

Cahill, Lisa Sowle. "Toward Global Ethics." *Theological Studies* 63 (2002): 324–44.

Calvez, Jean-Yves, SJ, and J. Perrin, SJ, *The Church and Social Justice.* Chicago: Henry Regnery, 1961).

Catholic Church, Pontificium Consilium de Iustitia et Pace. *Compendium of the Social Doctrine of the Church.* Vatican City: Veritas, 2005.

Christiansen, Drew. "Commentary on *Pacem in Terris.*" In Himes et al., *Modern Catholic Social Teaching.*

Clark, Meghan J. "The Complex but Necessary Union of Charity and Justice: Insights from the Vincentian Tradition for Contemporary Catholic Social Teaching" *Vincentian Heritage Journal,* Volume 31:2.2012, p. 25-39.

———. "Integrating Human Rights: Participation in John Paul II, Catholic Social Thought and Amartya Sen." *Political Theology* 8, no. 3 (2007): 299–317.

———. "Love of God and Neighbor: Living Charity in Aquinas' Ethics," *New Blackfriars* 92, no. 1040 (July 2011): 415–30. Clarke, W. Norris. *Person and Being*. Milwaukee, WI: Marquette University Press, 1993.

Coleman, John A. *One Hundred Years of Catholic Social Thought: Celebration and Challenge*. Maryknoll, NY: Orbis, 1991.

Coleman, John A., and William F. Ryan, eds. *Globalization and Catholic Social Thought: Present Crisis, Future Hope*. Toronto: Novalis; Maryknoll, NY: Orbis, 2005.

Cunningham, David S. "Participation as a Trinitarian Virtue: Challenging the Relational Consensus." *Toronto Journal of Theology* 14, no. 1 (1998): 7–25.

Curran, Charles E. *Catholic Social Teaching, 1891–Present: A Historical, Theological, and Ethical Analysis*. Moral Traditions Series. Washington, DC: Georgetown University Press, 2002.

———. *The Moral Theology of Pope John Paul II*. Moral Traditions Series. Washington, DC: Georgetown University Press, 2005.

Curran, Charles E., and Richard A. McCormick. *Official Catholic Social Teaching*. Readings in Moral Theology. New York: Paulist, 1986.

Cruft, Rowan. "Human Rights and Positive Duties." Response to *World Poverty and Human Rights*. *Ethics & International Affairs* 19, no. 1 (2006): 29–37.

Daly, Daniel J. "Structures of Virtue and Vice." *New Blackfriars* 92 (2011): 341–57.

Davies, Brian, OFM. *The Thought of Thomas Aquinas*. Oxford: Clarendon, 1993.

Deck, Allan Figueroa, SJ. "Commentary on *Populorum Progressio* (Development of Peoples)." In Himes et al., *Modern Catholic Social Teaching*.

De la Torre, Miguel, *Doing Christian Ethics From the Margins*. Mary knoll, NY: Orbis, 2004.

Donahue, John R. "The 'Parable' of the Sheep and the Goats: A Challenge to Christian Ethics." *Theological Studies* 47, no. 1 (1986): 3–31.

Doran, Kevin. *Solidarity: A Synthesis of Personalism and Communalism in the Thought of Karol Wojtyla/John Paul II*. American University Studies. Series 7, Theology and Religion, vol. 190. New York: Peter Lang, 1996.

Dorr, Donal. *Option for the Poor: A Hundred Years of Vatican Social Teaching*. Maryknoll, NY: Orbis, 1992.

———. "Solidarity and Integral Human Development." In *The Logic of Solidarity: Commentaries on Pope John Paul II's Encyclical "On Social Concern,"* edited by Gregory Baum and Robert Ellsberg, 143–54. Maryknoll, NY: Orbis, 1989.

Duffy, Regis, OFM, and Angelus Gambatese, OFM, eds. *Made in God's Image: The Catholic Vision of Human Dignity.* New York: Paulist, 1999.

Dulles, Avery Cardinal, SJ. "Indirect Mission of the Church to Politics." *Villanova Law Review* 52, no. 2 (2007): 241–52.

Farley, Margaret A., RSM. *Compassionate Respect: A Feminist Approach to Medical Ethics.* Milwaukee, WI: Paulist, 2002.

———. "New Patterns of Relationship: Beginnings of a Moral Revolution." *Theological Studies* 36, no. 4 (1975): 627–46.

Farmer, Paul. *Pathologies of Power: Health, Human Rights, and the New War on the Poor.* Berkeley: University of California Press, 2005.

Fox, Patricia. *God as Communion: John Zizioulas, Elizabeth Johnson, and the Retrieval of the Symbol of the Triune God.* Collegeville, MN: Liturgical Press, 2001.

Francis, Pope. "Address of His Holiness Pope Francis to Participants in the 38th Conference of the Food and Agriculture Organization of the United Nations (FAO)." June 20, 2013. http://www.vatican.va/holy_father/francesco/speeches/2013/june/documents/papa-francesco_20130620_38-sessione-fao_en.html.

———. "Address of Pope Francis." Visit to the community of Varginha (Manguinhos), Brazil. July 25, 2013. http://www.vatican.va/holy_father/francesco/speeches/2013/july/documents/papa-francesco_20130725_gmg-comunita-varginha_en.html.

———. "The Globalization of Indifference." Address at Lampedusa. July 8, 2013. http://en.radiovaticana.va/news/2013/07/08/pope_on_lampedusa:_%E2%80%9Cthe_globalization_of_indifference%E2%80%9 en1-708541.

Freedman, LP, RJ Waldman, dePinho, ME Wirth, AMR Chowdhury, and A Rosenfield, *Who's got the power? Transforming health systems for women and children.* Millennial Project: Task force on Child Health and Maternal Health (Oxford: Earthscan, 2005).

Friedman, Milton. *Capitalism and Freedom.* Chicago: University of Chicago Press, 2002.

Friedman, Milton and Rose. *Free to Choose: A Personal Statement.* New York: Mariner, 1990.

Garrett, S. M. Review of *The Liberating Image: The Imago Dei in Genesis 1*, by J. Richard Middleton, *Trinity Journal* 27, no. 2 (2006): 339–40.

Gilleman, Gerard, SJ. *Primacy of Charity in Moral Theology*. Westminster: Newman Press, 1959.

Glendon, Mary Ann. *A World Made New: Eleanor Roosevelt and the Universal Declaration of Human Rights*. New York: Random House, 2001.

Goizueta, Roberto S. *Caminemos con Jesus: Toward a Hispanic/Latino Theology of Accompaniment*. Maryknoll, NY: Orbis, 2002.

Government of Sudan, Federal Ministry of Health, Primary Health Care General Directorate, Mother and Child Health Directorate, "Road Map for Reducing Maternal and Newborn Mortality in Sudan (2010–2015)," December 2009; submitted to UNFPA by the Sudanese government, http://www.unfpa.org/sowmy/resources/docs/library/R101_MOHSudan_2010_MNMR_RoadMap_06Jan10.doc

Gregg, Samuel. *Challenging the Modern World: Karol Wojtyla/John Paul II and the Development of Catholic Social Teaching*. Religion, Politics, and Society in the New Millennium. Lanham, MD: Lexington, 1999.

———. "Deus caritas Est: The Social Message of the Pope," *Economic Affairs* Volume 26, Issue 2, pages 55–59 (June 2006).

Grenz, Stanley J. "The Social God and the Relational Self: Toward a Theology of the Imago Dei in the Postmodern Context." In *Personal Identity in Theological Perspective*, edited by Richard Lints, Michael S. Horton, and Mark R. Talbot, 70–92. Grand Rapids, MI: Eerdmans, 2006.

Gunton, Colin E. "Trinity, Ontology and Anthropology: Towards a Renewal of the Doctrine of the Imago Dei." In *Persons, Divine and Human*, edited by Christoph Schwöbel and Colin E. Gunton, 47–61. Edinburgh: T & T Clark, 1991.

Harrison, Nonna V. "Zizioulas on Communion and Otherness." *St. Vladimir's Theological Quarterly* 42, nos. 3–4 (1998): 273–300.

Hellwig, Monika. "The Quest for Common Ground in Human Rights: A Catholic Reflection." In *Human Rights in the Americas*, edited by Alfred Hennelly and John Langan, 159–66. Washington, DC: Georgetown University Press, 1982.

Herrick, Jennifer A. *Trinitarian Intelligibility—an Analysis of Contemporary Discussions: An Investigation of Western Academic Trinitarian Theology of Late Twentieth Century*: Boca Raton, Florida: Universal, 2007.

Himes, Kenneth R., OFM. "Commentary on *Justitia in Mundo* (Justice in the World)." In Himes et al., *Modern Catholic Social Teaching*.

———. "Globalization with a Human Face: Catholic Social Teaching and Globalization." *Theological Studies* 69, no. 2 (2008): 269–89.

Himes, Kenneth R., Lisa Sowle Cahill, Charles E. Curran, David Hollenbach, and Thomas Shannon, eds. *Modern Catholic Social Teaching: Commentaries and Interpretations.* Washington, DC: Georgetown University Press, 2005.

Himes, Michael J., and Kenneth R. Himes. *Fullness of Faith: The Public Significance of Theology.* New York: Paulist, 1993.Holland, Joe. *Modern Catholic Social Teaching: The Popes Confront the Industrial Age 1740-1958.* New York: Paulist, 2003.

Hollenbach, David, SJ. *Claims in Conflict: Retrieving and Renewing the Catholic Human Rights Tradition.* Woodstock Studies 4. New York: Paulist, 1979.

———. *The Common Good and Christian Ethics.* New Studies in Christian Ethics 22. Cambridge: Cambridge University Press, 2002.

———. *The Global Face of Public Faith: Politics, Human Rights, and Christian Ethics.* Moral Traditions Series. Washington, DC: Georgetown University Press, 2003.

———. "Solidarity, Development, and Human Rights: The African Challenge." *Journal of Religious Ethics* 25, no. 2 (1998): 305–17.

International Theological Commission. "Communion and Stewardship: Human Persons Created in the Image of God." 2004. http://www.vatican.va/roman_curia/congregations/cfaith/cti_documents/rc_con_cfaith_doc_20040723_communion-stewardship_en.html.

John Paul II, Pope. *Centesimus Annus.* Encyclical Letter. May 1, 1991. http://www.vatican.va/holy_father/john_paul_ii/encyclicals/documents/hf_jp-ii_enc_01051991_centesimus-annus_en.html.

———. "Development and Solidarity: Two Keys to Peace." Message for the Celebration of the World Day of Peace. January 1, 1987. http://www.vatican.va/holy_father/john_paul_ii/messages/peace/documents/hf_jp-ii_mes_19861208_xx-world-day-for-peace_en.html.

———. *Laborem Exercens.* Encyclical Letter. September 14, 1981. http://www.vatican.va/holy_father/john_paul_ii/encyclicals/documents/hf_jp-ii_enc_14091981_laborem-exercens_en.html.

———. *Sollicitudo Rei Socialis.* Encyclical Letter. December 30, 1987. http://www.vatican.va/holy_father/john_paul_ii/encyclicals/documents/hf_jp-ii_enc_30121987_sollicitudo-rei-socialis_en.html.

John XXIII, Pope. *Mater et Magistra.* Encyclical Letter on Christianity and Social Progress. May 15, 1961. http://www.vatican.va/holy_father/john_xxiii/encyclicals/documents/hf_j-xxiii_enc_15051961_mater_en.html.

———. *Pacem in Terris*. Encyclical Letter on Establishing Universal Peace in Truth, Justice, Charity, and Liberty. April 11, 1963. http://www.vatican.va/holy_father/john_xxiii/encyclicals/documents/hf_j-xxiii_enc_11041963_pacem_en.html.

Johnson, Elizabeth A., CSJ. *Consider Jesus: Waves of Renewal in Christology*. New York: Crossroad, 1990.

———. *Quest for the Living God: Mapping Frontiers in the Theology of God*. New York: Continuum, 2007.

———. *She Who Is: The Mystery of God in a Feminist Theological Perspective*. New York: Crossroad, 1992.

———. "Trinity: To Let the Symbol Sing Again." *Theology Today* 54, no. 3 (1997): 298–311.

Kant, Immanuel. *Grounding for the Metaphysics of Morals*. Translated by James W. Ellington. Indianapolis, IN: Hackett, 1993.

Keenan, James, SJ. "Virtue of Prudence," in *The Ethics of Aquinas*. Edited by Stephen J. Pope. Moral Traditions Series. Washington, DC: Georgetown University Press, 2002

Kent, Bonnie. "Habits and Virtues (Ia IIae, qq. 49–70)." In Pope, *The Ethics of Aquinas*.

Kerr, Fergus. "Taylor's Moral Ontology." In Abbey, *Charles Taylor*.

Ki-Moon, Ban. "A Life of Dignity for All: Accelerating Progress towards the Millennium Development Goals and Advancing the United Nations Development Agenda beyond 2015." United Nations Secretary General's Report. July 26, 2013. http://www.un.org/millenniumgoals/pdf/A%20Life%20of%20Dignity%20for%20All.pdf.

King, Jr., Martin Luther. *Measure of a Man*. Minneapolis, MN: Fortress Press, 2001

LaCugna, Catherine M. *God for Us: The Trinity and Christian Life*. San Francisco: HarperSanFrancisco, 1991.

Lamoureux, Patricia A. "Commentary on *Laborem Exercens* (On Human Work)." In Himes et al., *Modern Catholic Social Teaching*.

Lapsley, Jacqueline E. "Friends with God? Moses and the Possibility of Covenantal Friendship." *Interpretation* 58, no. 2 (2004): 117–29.

Levenson, Jon D. "The Davidic Covenant and Its Modern Interpreters." *Catholic Biblical Quarterly* 41, no. 2 (1979): 205–19.

Little, GA, W Keenan, S Niermeyer, N Singhal, and J Lawn, "Neonatal nursing and helping babies breathe: an effective intervention to decrease global neonatal mortality." *Pediatrics* (2010) 126 (5). P. 82-3. Available at:

http://www.helpingbabiesbreathe.org/docs/
Neonatal%20Nursing%202011.pdf

Lozano, R, H Wang, KJ Foreman, JKRajaratnam, M Naghavi, JR Marcus, L Dwyer-Lindgren,KT Lofgren, D Phillips, C Atkinson, AD Lopez, Christopher, and JL Muray, "Progress towards Millennium Development Goals 4 and 5 on maternal and child mortality: an updated systematic analysis." *The Lancet* (24 September 2011) Vol. 378, Issue 9797, Pages 1139-1165.

Miguez Bonino, José. "A Covenant of Life: A Meditation on Genesis 9:1-17." *Ecumenical Review* 33, no. 4 (1981): 341–45.

Mahoney, Jack, SJ. *The Challenge of Human Rights: Their Origin, Development, and Significance.* Malden, MA: Blackwell, 2007.

Maritain, Jacques. Introduction to *Human Rights: Commentaries and Interpretations*, edited by UNESCO. New York: Columbia University Press, 1949.

———. *Man and the State.* Washington, DC: Catholic University of America Press, 1998.

Maritain, Jacques, and John J. Fitzgerald. *The Person and the Common Good.* Notre Dame, IN: University of Notre Dame Press, 1966.

McHugh, Francis P., Samuel M. Natale, John Schachinger, and Brian Rothschild, eds. *Things Old and New: Catholic Social Teaching Revisited.* Lanham, MD: University Press of America; London: Oxford Philosophy Trust, 1993.

Mich, Marvin L. K. *Catholic Social Teaching and Movements.* Mystic, CT: Twenty-Third, 1998.

Moltmann, Jürgen. *Experiences in Theology: Ways and Forms of Christian Theology* [Erfahrungen theologischen Denkens]. Minneapolis: Fortress Press, 2000.

———. *On Human Dignity: Political Theology and Ethics.* Philadelphia: Fortress Press, 1984.

"Multi-Dimensional Poverty Index." United Nations Development Programme, Human Development Reports. http://hdr.undp.org/en/statistics/mpi/.

Nelson, Eric. "From Primary Goods to Capabilities: Distributive Justice and the Problem of Neutrality." *Political Theory* 36, no. 1 (2008): 93–122.

O'Brien, David J., and Thomas A. Shannon, eds. *Catholic Social Thought: The Documentary Heritage.* Maryknoll, NY: Orbis, 1992.

O'Neill, Onora. "Global Justice: Whose Obligations?" In *The Ethics of Assistance: Morality and the Distant Needy*, edited by Deen K. Chatterjee, 242–60. Cambridge: Cambridge University Press, 2004.

Okin, Susan Moller. "Poverty, Well-Being, and Gender: What Counts, Who's Heard?" *Philosophy & Public Affairs* 31, no. 3 (2003): 280–316.

Paul VI, Pope. *Populorum Progressio*. In O'Brien and Shannon, *Catholic Social Thought*.

Pieris, Aloysius. "The Catholic Theology of Human Rights and the Covenant Theology of Human Responsibilities." *Dialogue* 30 (2003): 104–25.

Pinkard, Terry. "Taylor and the History of Philosophy." In Abbey, *Charles Taylor*.

Pogge, Thomas. "Are we Violating the Human Rights of the World's Poor?" *Yale Human Rights and Development Law Journal* 14, no.2. (2012), p. 1-33.

———. "Assisting the Global Poor." In *The Ethics of Assistance: Morality and the Distant Needy*, edited by Deen K. Chatterjee. Cambridge: Cambridge University Press, 2004.

———. "Priorities of Global Justice." *Metaphilosophy* 32 (2001): 6–24.

———. *World Poverty and Human Rights: Cosmopolitan Responsibilities and Reforms*. Cambridge: Polity, 2002.

Pope, Stephen J. *The Ethics of Aquinas*. Moral Traditions Series. Washington, DC: Georgetown University Press, 2002.

Porter, Jean. "The Search for a Global Ethic." Theological Studies 62 (2001): 105–21.

Rahner, Karl, SJ. "Person." In *Encyclopedia of Theology: The Concise Sacramentum Mundi*, by Karl Rahner. New York: Seabury Press, 1975.

———. *Theology of Freedom*, in *Theological Investigations*. Vol. 6, 178–96.

Rajaratnam, Julie Knoll et al. "Neonatal, Postnatal, Childhood, and Under-5 Mortality for 187 Countries, 1970–2010: A Systematic Analysis of Progress towards Millennium Development Goal 4," *Lancet* 375 (2010), doi: 10.1016/S0140-6736(10)60703-9.

Rand, Ayn. *"The Objectivist Ethics." Paper delivered at the University of Wisconsin Symposium, "Ethics in Our Time," in Madison, Wisconsin, on February 9, 1961. Later published in The Virtue of Selfishness (1961).*

Rendtorff, Rolf. "'Covenant' as a Structuring Concept in Genesis and Exodus." *Journal of Biblical Literature* 108, no. 3 (1989): 385–93.

Rudman, Stanley. *The Concept of the Person and Christian Ethics*. Cambridge: Cambridge University Press, 1997.

Ruston, Roger. *Human Rights and the Image of God*. London: SCM, 2004.

Schockenhoff, Eberhard. *Law and Human Dignity: Universal Ethics in an Historical World*. Washington DC: Catholic University Press, 2003.

Schweiker, William. "The Good and Moral Identity: A Theological Ethical Response to Charles Taylor's 'Sources of the Self.'" *Journal of Religion* 72, no. 4 (1992): 560–72.

Scirghi, Thomas J., SJ, "The Trinity: A Model for Belonging in Contemporary Society." *Ecumenical Review* 54, no. 3 (2002): 333–42.

Sen, Amartya. "Capability and Well-Being." In *The Quality of Life*, edited by Martha S. Nussbaum and Amartya Sen. Oxford: Oxford University Press, 1993.

———. *Development as Freedom*. New York: Anchor, 1999.

———. "Elements of a Theory of Human Rights." *Philosophy and Public Affairs* 32, no. 4 (2004): 315–56.

———. "Human Rights and Capabilities." *Journal of Human Devleopment* 6, no. 2 (July 2005).

———. *The Idea of Justice*. Cambridge, MA: Harvard University Press, 2009.

———. "Identity and Violence: The Illusion of Destiny." *Zeitschrift fuer philosophische Forschung* 61, no. 4 (2007): 537–40.

———. *Inequality Reexamined*. Oxford: Oxford University Press, 1995.

———. "Justice across Borders." In *Global Justice and Transnational Politics*, edited by Pablo De Greiff and Ciaran Cronin. Cambridge, MA: MIT Press, 2002.

———. *Rationality and Freedom*. Cambridge, MA: Belknap Press of Harvard University Press, 2002.

———. "Social Choice Theory and Justice." In *Constructions of Practical Reason: Interviews on Moral and Political Philosophy*, edited by Herlinde Pauer-Studer. Stanford, CA: Stanford University Press, 2003.

———. "Symposium on Amartya Sen's Philosophy: 4 Reply." *Economics and Philosophy* 17, no. 1 (2001): 51-66.

———. "What Do We Want from a Theory of Justice?" *Journal of Philosophy* 103, no. 5 (2006): 215–38.

Sibley, Angus. *The "Poisoned Spring" of Economic Libertarianism: Menger, Mises, Hayek, Rothbard; a Critique from Catholic Social Teaching of the "Austrian School" of Economics*. Washington, DC: Pax Romana, 2011.

Simon, John, Charles W. Powers, and Jon P. Gunnemann. "The Responsibilities of Corporations and Their Owners." In *The Ethical Investor: Universities and Corporate Responsibility*. New Haven, CT: Yale University Press, 1972.

Smith, Nicholas H. *Charles Taylor: Meaning, Morals, and Modernity*. Cambridge, UK: Polity, 2002.

Sweeney, Eileen. "Vice and Sin (Ia IIae, qq. 71–89)." In Pope, *The Ethics of Aquinas*.

Synod of Bishops. *Justitia in Mundo*. In O'Brien and Shannon, *Catholic Social Thought*.

Taylor, Charles. "Charles Taylor Replies." In *Philosophy in an Age of Pluralism: The Philosophy of Charles Taylor in Question*, edited by James Tully. New York: Cambridge Univ Press, 1994.

———. *The Ethics of Authenticity*. Cambridge, MA: Harvard University Press, 1992.

———. *Human Agency and Language*. Philosophical Papers 1. New York: Cambridge University Press, 1985.

———. *Modern Social Imaginaries*. Public Planet Books. Durham, NC: Duke University Press, 2004.

———. *Philosophical Arguments*. Cambridge, MA: Harvard University Press, 1995.

———. *Philosophy and the Human Sciences*. Philosophical Papers 2. Cambridge: Cambridge University Press, 1985.

———. *A Secular Age*. Cambridge, MA: Belknap Press of Harvard University Press, 2007.

———. *Sources of the Self: The Making of the Modern Identity*. Cambridge, MA: Harvard University Press, 1989.

———. "Two Theories of Modernity." *Hastings Center Report* 25, no. 2 (1995): 24–34.

Taylor, Charles, and Amy Gutmann. *Multiculturalism and the Politics of Recognition: An Essay*. Princeton, NJ: Princeton University Press, 1992.

Taylor, Charles, and James Heft. *A Catholic Modernity?: Charles Taylor's Marianist Award Lecture, with Responses by William M. Shea, Rosemary Luling Haughton, George Marsden, and Jean Bethke Elshtain*. New York: Oxford University Press, 1999.

Towner, W. Sibley. "Clones of God: Genesis 1:26-28 and the Image of God in the Hebrew Bible." *Interpretation* 59, no. 4 (2005): 341–56.

UNICEF. "State of the World's Children 2009" http://www.unicef.org/protection/SOWC09-FullReport-EN.pdf,

United Nations. "Declaration on the Right to Development," 1986, un.org/documents/ga/res/41/a411/28.htm

———."Universal Declaration of Human Rights" (1948), http://www.un.org/en/documents/udhr/

United Nations Development Program (UNDP). *Human Development Report 2000.* http://hdr.undp.org/en/content/human-development-report-2000

———. *Human Development Report 2003.* http://hdr.undp.org/en/content/human-development-report-2003

———. *Millennium Development Goals Report 2012.* New York: United Nations, 2012. http://www.un.org/millenniumgoals/pdf/MDG%20Report%202012.pdf.

———. *The Rise of the South: Human Progress in a Diverse World.* Human Development Report 2013. http://www.undp.org/content/dam/undp/library/corporate/HDR/2013GlobalHDR/English/HDR2013%20Report%20English.pdf.

United Nations General Assembly. "Implementing the Responsibility to Protect: Report of the Secretary General," January 12, 2009. http://responsibilitytoprotect.org/implementing%20the%20rtop.pdf.

United Nations High Commissioner for Refugees. "*Protecting Refugees and the Role of the UNHCR,* 2007–2008" (Geneva: UNHCR, 2007). http://www.unhcr.org/49eecf142.html

United Nations Office of Human Rights. Right to Development Booklet, http://ohchr.org/documents/issues/develop[pment/RTD_booklet_en.pdf

Vatican II. *Gaudium et Spes.* Pastoral Constitution on the Church in the Modern World. December 7, 1965. http://www.vatican.va/archive/hist_councils/ii_vatican_council/documents/vat-ii_cons_19651207_gaudium-et-spes_en.html.

Verstraeten, Johan. "Rethinking Catholic Social Thought as Tradition," in *Catholic Social Thoguht: Twighlight or Rennaissance?* Edited by. J.S. Boswell, F. P. McHugh, and J. Verstraeten. Leuven: Leuven University Press, 2000.

Von Hayek, Friedrich. *Individualism and Economic Order.* Chicago: University of Chicago Press, 1948.

———. *The Constitution of Liberty.* London: Routlege Press, 1960.

Wall, S. et al. "Neonatal Resuscitation in Low-Resource Settings: What, Who, and How to Overcome Challenges to Scale Up?" *International Journal of Gynecology & Obstetrics* 107, suppl. (October 2009): S47–S64.

Weigel, George. "*Caritas in Veritate* in Red and Gold." *National Review,* July 7, 2009.

Wojtyla, Karol. *The Acting Person: A Contribution to Phenomenological Anthropology.* Translated by Andrzej Potocki. Boston: D. Reidel, 1979.

Chapter 7 available at http://www.angelfire.com/music5/sheetmusic4free/ActingPerson/CHAPTER_SEVEN.htm.

———. *Catholic Social Thought from Lublin: Person and Community, Selected Essays.* New York: Peter Lang, 1993.

———. *Love and Responsibility.* New York: Farrar, Straus and Giroux, 1981.

———. *Toward a Philosophy of Praxis.* New York: Crossroad, 1981.

Wolicka, Elżbieta. "Participation in Community: Wojtyla's Social Anthropology." *Communio* 3, no. 2 (1981): 108–18.

Woodall, G. J. Review of *The Logic of Solidarity: Commentaries on Pope John Paul II's Encyclical 'On Social Concerns'* by Gregory Baum, *New Blackfriars* 73, no. 862 (1992): 410–13.

World Federalist Movement, Institute for Global Policy. "Summary of the *Responsibility to Protect*: The Report of the International Commission on Intervention and State Sovereignty (ICISS)." Responsibility to Protect–Engaging Civil Society Project. n.d. http://www.responsibilitytoprotect.org/files/R2PSummary.pdf.

World Health Organization. "Mortality and Burdens of Disease." *World Health Statistics* 2009, http://www.who.int/whosis/whostat/EN_WHS09_Table1.pdf.

Yeager, D. M. "Emerging Issues in Human Rights." *Journal of Religious Ethics* 26, no. 2 (1998): 269–328.

Zizioulas, John D. *Being as Communion: Studies in Personhood and the Church.* London: Darton, Longman & Todd, 1985.

———. "Communion and Otherness." *St. Vladimir's Theological Quarterly* 38, no. 4 (1994): 347–61.

———. *Communion and Otherness: Further Studies in Personhood and the Church.* Edited by Paul McPartlan. New York: T & T Clark, 2006.

Index of Names

Index of Subjects

CPSIA information can be obtained at www.ICGtesting.com
Printed in the USA
LVOW12s0743190614

390431LV00010B/9/P